Contents

About the author

Toni Battison is a trained nurse who has had considerable practical and teaching experience during her career working with older people and carers. She has worked as a District Nursing Sister, a Health Promotion Adviser, a Lecturer for a Certificate in Health Education course, and as the manager of a charity. She is now retired from these external roles and works part time on her freelance health education work. Toni has written many publications promoting good health, and contributes to local radio. She is an Associate Member of the Guild of Health Writers.

Toni has always been concerned about the need to support carers and patients to enable them to get the best from local and national services, as she believes people obtain great benefit from being able to help themselves. While working for the Cambridge and Huntingdon Health Authority, she helped create an information centre for patients and visitors at Addenbrooke's Hospital and, with other carers, started the Telephone Information Line for Carers of Elderly People in the Cambridge area. She was joint winner of the Ian Nichol Prize for Health Promotion in 1990 and 1992 for these projects.

Toni lives near Cambridge with her husband, and has three grown up daughters. She is the main carer for her mother (in her late 80s) who lives with her. In the past, she helped her mother care for her father, following a series of strokes and epilepsy, until he died at home. Her experience of caring for her parents has given a personal perspective that complements her professional role.

Acknowledgements

The author thanks the many people – carers, friends and colleagues – who have contributed valuable help and advice throughout the production of this book. In particular:

Dr Stephen Webster, Consultant Emeritus, Department of Medicine for the Elderly, Addenbrooke's Hospital, Cambridge who commented on the material and provided the Introduction.

Staff members at Age Concern England who were particularly helpful include Richard Holloway, Vinnette Marshall, and Sue Henning, while Richenda Milton-Thompson worked on the manuscript in a freelance editorial capacity.

A number of people, some of them unknown to me, reviewed the draft material and made important suggestions to help improve the text.

In addition I thank all the national and local organisations that offer information and support to carers in the broadest sense, whose materials have helped to inform and influence my thinking.

Introduction

It is our ability to think, remember and plan that is perhaps our soul, or at least makes us responsible adults. The threat of losing our memory, our identity and our ability to manage our own affairs is, to most of us, the greatest disaster that may overtake us. With our mind intact, many of us feel that we might be able to cope with physical disability, if the right help were available. However, if it were our memory and ability to think that was lost, how would we even know if we were coping?

Unfortunately, memory loss becomes more common with advancing years. But will still affect only a minority of older people. When it does happen, though, it is frightening for both the victim and the onlookers. Just reflect how frustrated and impatient you can feel when you have difficulty remembering something familiar or an acquaintance's name, even though you feel it is as familiar as your own face. Again, consider the anxiety you experience when you cannot find you car keys, your handbag or wallet – even when you know they are safe and can't be far away.

Memory is important to us all and we should try to protect, cherish, improve and enjoy this important asset. However, we must also be honest and sensible if we discover it is beginning to let us down. The first step in all coping mechanisms is to recognise the problem, and then devise tactics and strategies to overcome and minimise the defect or loss.

This book is full of commonsense advice about how to structure our lives (or the life of another) in such a manner that any damage is as limited as possible. If your memory is failing, it needs the security and peace of mind that can be provided by adjustment to the environment to ensure stability, happiness and tranquillity. Attention must be paid to both the internal environment – in particular to general health and happiness – as well as to the outside world. For many older people, that is all that may be required.

Unfortunately, the early memory loss can sometimes be a harbinger of something more sinister – dementia. Discussing the problem with your GP is important as he or she will be well placed to help point you in the direction of supporting agencies and act as a guide through any future difficulties. Dementia is not just a single condition: some forms (only a few, unfortunately) can be reversed. However, more can be slowed down in their progress by the early and careful use of new drugs. Hopefully, new and more effective interventions will become available as a consequence of increased research into the all forms of dementia and general openness about the disease.

At the end of the book, there is advice specifically directed towards carers of very dependent people. Don't be alarmed: as a carer, you may not need to provide that level of help, but it has to be there for the less fortunate. In the same vein, don't be alarmed by the inclusion of advice about Enduring Powers of Attorney or Advance Directives. These are wise precautions for everybody to take – if they are never used, then no harm is done. But should they be needed and used, then harm may be prevented. By discussing these matters with potential carers at an early stage, the 'patient' can play an important role in the training and preparation of their future carers and protectors. Trying to think ahead may help to minimise the consequences of a failing memory. Hence the justification for this excellent book.

Stephen Webster MA, MD, FRCP
Consultant Emeritus, Department of Medicine for the Elderly,
Addenbrooke's Hospital, Cambridge

1 What is memory loss?

Any health problem, whatever its cause, is reason for concern. Fortunately, advances in medical care offer an abundance of treatments, services and products, which at best halt the decline in health-related problems and, on the whole make us well again. To get the picture think about eye-tests and spectacles, hearing tests and hearing aids, antibiotics for infection, pain-killing drugs for discomfort, hip replacement surgery and so on .... This huge range of care has led to high expectations that, whatever the illness, something can be done to make it better. Unfortunately, this will not always be the case. Loss of memory is one example of a condition for which a prescription from the doctor or a visit to a hospital clinic cannot provide a simple result.

If memory loss has become a problem for a close relative or friend, to a level that is affecting their daily welfare, you might be wondering what the future holds. The prospect is not completely bleak. Carers need not be totally disheartened because quite a lot can be done to improve the day-to-day situation of someone whose memory is failing. At present there are no standard, quick-fix solutions or golden promises that full memory function could be regained. But, with help and support, a general improvement is often achievable.

The medical term for memory loss is 'amnesia'. Loss of memory can be a temporary or permanent difficulty, can take many forms and there are many causes. In some cases the problem improves with time, for example, when the root cause is a treatable physical illness, or an accident such as a blow to the head, or where, for psychological reasons, the person might be trying to block out an unpleasant, emotional memory. These types of memory loss will not be covered by this book, except where they are drawn upon to illustrate a point. Neither is the book designed to cover the type of memory loss found in people who are suffering from clinical dementia.

Researchers looking at alteration in mental function have identified gradual changes in ability as people age. In particular, the capacity to remember names seems to be affected by age. This is the type of memory loss with which this book is primarily concerned. The following chapters offer carers a simple explanation of how memory works, information about the various tests and treatments that their relative might receive if further investigation is necessary, some practical advice about various issues – including keeping their relative safe and sorting out everyday affairs – and helpful guidelines about making best use of existing memory function. The final chapter is especially about you, as a carer. If you are new to this role and have never applied this description to yourself before, you may wish to read this chapter first and view it as an introduction to your current situation.

It might appear that the book is being less than honest in that it starts by implying that memory loss should not be viewed as a huge problem but in later chapters offers information about caring for a dependent person. It is never possible to forecast how the health of any individual person will progress. This type of supporting material has been included for those carers who might find it useful, either at the present time or at some stage in the future. It is not intended as an omen of things to come.

Listening to older people (and their relatives) it is commonplace to hear them grumble about how their memory is 'playing them up', how it can 'no longer be relied upon' and how they are frequently embarrassed by 'inevitable blunders'. In the best case, mistakes are 'laughed off', but behind the humour often conceals a person who feels humiliated by the gaffes, who is deeply worried about dealing with everyday life and fearful for the future. When memory begins to falter perceptibly, the first anxiety for all concerned is often the possibility of approaching dementia, with Alzheimer's disease doubtless topping the list. It is true that this illness, with its more severe forms of memory loss, does start off with symptoms of poor memory. However, if your relative's memory lapses involve nothing worse than losing their door keys, forgetting names and generally mis-remembering details from recent conversations, then it is very unlikely that their problem is being caused by impending dementia. You can also rest assured that, if consulted, their doctor will certainly do the necessary checks to rule out all forms of dementia.

Dr Stuart, Consultant Geriatrician

'Although dementia clearly increases with age, we should never forget that most people do *not* dement.'

It is a common mistake to lump together all versions of memory failure as a single problem, but in reality this is rarely the case. People mis-remember for many different reasons. Memory function is explained more clearly below, but there isn't one big pot in our brain which is used to store a complete 'memory soup' of everything that enters the system from which random memories are later extracted. The system is extremely complex, the ability to remember differs from person to person and, for some people, the system goes wrong. Your relative might remember lots of details about their school friends in the same class, but nothing about who sat next to them at the day centre on the previous day. Another older person might have an excellent memory for recalling historical facts but is hopeless at retrieving the trivia. Before

3

exploring aspects of malfunction, it is worth taking a look at normal memory performance to help explain some of the deficiencies.

Normal memory function

The memory is a very complex instrument and it is one element crucial to our ability to function as an independent person. The majority of people do not possess, or need in everyday life, a super, high grade memory capacity; fortunately for society, most of us manage well with a lesser version. We might wish for a better memory, just as many of us would like to be thinner or taller, but circumstances have dictated otherwise. However, we do need a level of competence that permits us to go about our daily business safely and sensibly. For an older person with a degree of memory loss, this means being able to cope confidently within the scope of their reducing power.

The main factor controlling memory function is the 'neuro-physiological process', the method by which the human brain sorts out the enormous input of information continually bombarding its systems. Roughly translated, this means 'the inner workings of the brain and nervous system' (explained simply below). The easiest way to understand the process is to think about memory as working in three stages, whereby information is received, stored and then, at a later time, recalled. In this respect, the three-stage process is the same for everyone, but other factors also play a part in how our memory is trained to work. For example, cultural traditions exert a significant influence over the manner in which certain communities record information. In some societies heavy reliance is placed on visual memory, such as the techniques learned in complicated dance routines passed down through the generations. Other peoples have developed amazing aural abilities, ensuring that huge tracts of their history are preserved through human memory. Most Western cultures favour the written word as a way of storing information, whether for merely jotting down a few items on a shopping list or the long term recording of history. Where a person's reading and writing skills are not well developed, it often appears that their memory proficiency is far sharper. While visiting friends in an Eastern country the author was amazed when a travelling pedlar arrived at the house the day following our arrival, to show his wares to the visitors from England. He had been told many months earlier to come on that particular day.

Stage One: Registering information

This first stage in the memory process is where *every piece* of information, experienced by our bodies, is registered by the brain. For example, when we are introduced to a person whom we have never met before, our brain immediately starts to register facts: their name, hair colour, whether they are tall or short, and so on; or, the sounds, smells and sensations that continually waft around; or the discomfort of a headache. These details are transferred instantly to the part of the brain where preliminary memories are stored.

Stage Two: Storing information

The second stage comes into operation immediately, as the brain starts to process all new information. Initially, the details are put in temporary storage, into a holding file capable of retaining a limited amount of information only. This temporary file can keep about five to nine items at any moment, but nothing resides in this holding bay for very long. As new pieces of information enter at one end, older facts are discarded or moved on to more permanent areas, where further decisions are made. A group of psychologists experimenting with memory tests towards the end of the twentieth century drew the conclusion that short term memory function is divided into three areas with each section working together. The group described this particular piece of the process as our 'working memory' and named each part of the system after its purpose:

- the 'visuo-spacial sketch pad', where images are stored;
- the 'phonological loop', where speech-based material is processed; and
- the 'central executive' part, which organises and makes sense of the information temporarily stored in the other two areas.

Information put into the phonological loop is further processed in two steps. Words with no immediate value to us disappear within a few seconds, but things that we want to keep for a bit we 'rehearse'. This explains why someone with normal memory function is able to remember a sequence of numbers long enough to dial a new telephone number but would be unlikely to remember the exact digits half an hour later. It is also why we forget the names of new acquaintances very quickly, unless we take definite steps to store the details for future reference.

Every single item of information that enters our bodies goes through this process – smells and sounds, pain and pleasure, television programmes we see, places we visit, people we meet, the sad and happy emotions we experience. The storage sequence continues as our brain makes a decision about whether the latest input needs to be retained as a short or long term item. It may be difficult to comprehend the complexity of the process but *everything* that happens to us is analysed in detail, however minute, before a decision is taken to either discard or retain the memory. At this stage, most people have a favoured way in which they consciously store information, perhaps by repeating an address a few times or linking the title of a book to a colour or place, and this helps with future recall.

Sensibly, the majority of information received into the brain is not stored permanently because it has no long term value. You could call this short term space your memory's current account because, like money in this style of bank account, it merely passes through. To continue the analogy, your other memory area is used like a safe deposit box, because it is here that permanent memories are stored for long term retention. For most people this lasting bank of information is vast because scientists believe there is no known limit to the amount of detail that can be retained, whether factual or emotional, and normally this process continues throughout our lives. Imagine the colossal amount of information that has passed through, and therefore been stored permanently in, the brain of an eighty-year old person.

It is also believed that within our permanent storage area we use distinct sections to hold different types of information, rather than jumble it all in together. Factual information is labelled and stored in a different way from knowledge and skills, so instructions about how to ride a bike or read a book are kept separately from our stored list of telephone numbers.

Psychologists have identified and named five different types of memory storage:

- **Short-term** memory area, for information retained briefly – for example, conversations from earlier in the day, news events that are no longer newsworthy, mental arithmetic sums.
- **Procedural** memory for skills, such as how to bake a cake or play a particular sport, or musical instrument.
- **Episodic** memories covering personal events, such as family parties, the sadness you felt when a pet died, or the place where you sheltered during a particularly violent storm.
- **Semantic** memory covers the bulk of the information, facts and figures that you have stored as a result of your education and experience; for example, important rules covering language or historical details about your home town.
- **Prospective** memory for the jobs that you must remember to do in the future; for example, booking a dental appointment, telling your daughter that you need more soap or when to return your library books.

Scientists believe the ease and accuracy with which we later recall information depends to some extent on how we have organised our brain at this sifting stage, ie the way in which we label (identify) the memory for future retrieval. Inevitably, flaws occur in the system so that memories that are stored hastily, without a definite marker, are more difficult to recall than those stored clearly within defined categories. The value of categorising information into determined areas, such as 'taste', or 'work procedures' or 'holiday pictures', will be explained more fully in Chapter 3 when self-help strategies are discussed.

Stage Three: Recalling information

The final step explains how, in order to retrieve the necessary facts, we put the storage process into reverse action. The information required will be residing already in one of the memory banks, short or long term, however our brain has previously instructed. Conversations that took place the previous day will be held in our short term memory bank, whereas details of where we lived in childhood will be housed in one or more of the permanent stores. The recollection we are seeking then requires a trigger to bring it back up to the surface and where we search depends on the nature of the information to be retrieved. A question relating to the name of the house we lived in twenty years ago requires precise detail, so our brains search for the answer in a different box to that used if we had been asked a general question about the flowers we can picture growing in the garden. This example also demonstrates the complexity of the system, because it clearly illustrates how memories (about the same matter) are stored in different compartments, according to their purpose. The house name will have been retrieved from the 'semantic' box, because it is a historical fact, but the pleasurable memory of seeing the flowers will be drawn from the episodic box, because it comes from personal experience.

As you can imagine there are a vast number of 'boxes' so the process can never be entirely smooth running. It is at this searching stage we are all likely to encounter the occasional blip, when the detail we are seeking eludes us. The inability to dredge up precise detail, such as a name or a song tune, is a common phenomenon, whatever our age, and does not mean that we are starting to malfunction. Even such a minor glitch can cause extreme irritation; envisage then how frustrating it becomes for your relative when age-related memory loss impedes their efforts at retrieving all types of information.

Memories play tricks

Don't get too exasperated with your relative when they appear to mis-remember or you think that they are not trying hard enough, because the problem might not always be related to memory loss. Recalling abstract sensations, such as smells or sounds, can never be absolutely accurate and it doesn't really matter. However, it is also interesting that our brains are quite selective about what (and how) we choose to recall, even literal things, sometimes to suit our own purposes! Certain items of unquestionable fact, such as the colour of a person's eyes, cannot be altered. However, much of the information we store is open to tampering and the detail that gets reproduced is not always an exact replica of what went in. Over the years (or even in the short term) our brains subtly adapt and adjust the facts, often unconsciously without our being aware that this amendment has taken place. We might believe firmly that we are recalling and relating an incident precisely as it happened, but someone else amazes us by telling the same story in a different way. And how many times have we returned to a town after many years absence and been surprised by our apparent faulty memory. This ability to rearrange information, on a small or grand scale according to our perception of its value, is absolutely normal. We all do it! Sometimes we deliberately embellish the truth and at other times our brains make unconscious changes, after we have mulled over the facts, without conscious prompting.

How the brain works in the memory process

The brain directs all bodily functions and each operation is inter-related. Whenever action is taking place messages are communicated between the appropriate system (eg digestive, sensory) and the central nervous system, using an extremely complex configuration of electrical and chemical activity (neurons and neurotransmitters). Here is a very simple example: if you need a drink, your dry mouth sends a message to your brain which recognises the feeling (because it has previously memorised the sensation); another section of memory directs you to the places in the kitchen where the kettle and the necessary ingredients are kept, and so on … your brain has recalled the crucial set of tea-making skills from the memory bank where 'utilising instructions' are stored, and your mind does the rest. (A dog would go to its water bowl.) Any information passed around the body and throughout the brain does so via communication pathways using neurons and neurotransmitters, which link together all body cells. Scientists are fairly sure that long term memory connections are stored in a network pattern, between neurons, and scattered around the brain. When a memory is recalled, the identifying stimulus or trigger lights up a network of pathways leading to the appropriate storage section.

It is normal to forget

In the memory sequence described earlier (registering, storage and recall), the ability to forget or discard unwanted information is an important part of the process – a filter mechanism – designed to prevent our memory banks being cluttered by unnecessary detail. It is quite normal for information to be dumped very swiftly as it is superseded by more up-to-date facts and, from time to time, we get this wrong. We throw out something vital, or fail to store crucial details correctly by directing them to the wrong compartment. It is also normal for memories to become blurred, particularly when the details have lain unused for a long time, a bit like a curtain that fades in the sun. A steady decline in memory power is inevitable, something we must all learn to accept. In our younger days we recognise a memory failure (perhaps the memory we have retrieved is lacking in detail) and we find ways to compensate. This ability tends to be less sharp in older people.

What is likely to go wrong?

Dr Stuart, Consultant Geriatrician

'I believe that memory does change with age – we lose the speed and flexibility of youth, just as we do with our muscles and joints. However, there is some compensation through experience and self-knowledge. As a consequence most people do not have to worry.'

Like all systems, mechanical or otherwise, things do not always run smoothly. For many older people, the occasional memory mishap gradually becomes the norm, where forgetfulness prevails. The difference is that now they are less aware of the extent of the problem and the system fails to compensate. Poor memory function can be provoked by a number of external and internal factors. The list of exacerbating factors below is common to all age groups but they are likely to have a greater effect in older age.

For example:

■ difficulties in absorbing excess information (overload);
■ a troubled state of mind;
■ the effects of physical or mental disabilities;
■ impaired senses;
■ deterioration in the physiological process (the way the body works);
■ lifestyle changes.

Absorbing excess information

If senses are overloaded with too much information, it becomes more difficult to register detail or sort out the value of the new material and store the facts. The ability to take in the new information is made worse if everything happens at great speed. For example, if an older person goes to a busy shopping centre, the whirl of activity around them may be overwhelming as sights and sounds rush in and out of their temporary storage box, without being properly processed. A week later the whole episode might feel like a daze and they would manage to recall little about the event. On the other hand, a younger person who might have accompanied them would most probably be able describe quite accurately the shops visited and the purchases made. Similarly, an older person who is introduced to a steady stream of friends at a family gathering would be far less able than a younger relative, the following day, to match faces to names.

A troubled state of mind

In the same way that excess information scrambles the system, the memory process can also be influenced by a state of mind. People who feel stressed, anxious or depressed tend to function below par, which in turn affects their ability to concentrate and manage their memory systems. Over-anxious people worry about how they will cope; depressed people tend to have slower reactions and people who are stressed become more agitated. These various worries create internal distractions which prevent them focusing clearly on what is happening externally. An older person, who is already troubled by short term memory loss might then worsen and pay less attention because, once a pattern of not coping is established, apprehension triggers self doubt and fear increases anxiety. You may have noticed that your relative anticipates problems when approaching a new situation and frets over how they acted at previous events, fuelling their belief that they will not cope.

Physical and mental disabilities

Deterioration in either physical or mental health can reduce memory function because our bodies' systems are interactive and problems in one area can affect efficiency elsewhere. Chronic pain, debilitating illness or distressing mental health problems can each hamper the memory process. In most cases it is not the actual disease which creates the problem (although the site of a stroke might be crucial), but rather that any residual memory loss is made worse by the sapping effects of continual suffering and/or side effects of medication. Examples of ever-present ill health include diabetes, arthritis, heart disease and many other illnesses. Scientists have yet to establish any firm physical links, but the incidence is too common to be disregarded.

Impaired senses

The effects brought about by impaired senses are fairly easy to understand. The deterioration in hearing, vision and other senses, commonly felt by the majority of older people, is bound to contribute to their memory problems and their ability to store new material. Imperfect sight or loss of pitch in hearing means that any information received into the temporary storage area will be flawed and reduced. For example, someone no longer hearing correctly might pick up only half a sentence and, as many crucial words are missed, the sense becomes meaningless. People with poor hearing either stop listening at an early stage, or become agitated and fail to register facts correctly. Continually struggling to hear is tiring, so they frequently give up any attempt to be part of mixed conversation.

The trauma of impaired senses can have a knock-on effect. Loss of sight usually means older people read less, so their memory is less stretched by new information. A lowered sense of taste means their taste buds are no longer excited by fresh flavours. A person who cannot see well is less likely to walk about in a garden and smell the variety of perfumes; in consequence that that part of their memory storage will become under-used.

Changes in the physiological process

It is an indisputable fact that our bodies deteriorate as we age. Every physical system in the body, joints, muscles, digestion and circulation, performs less well. Likewise, mental aptitude and memory slow down and reaction times become sluggish. Each stage of the memory process takes longer to execute, partly because of natural degeneration and also because older people find it harder to concentrate on more than one activity, simultaneously. For example, if someone interrupts while they are already listening to the radio, the new conversation becomes the dominant focus of attention. Information from the radio continues to enter their temporary memory store, but the detail is lost immediately, without being absorbed. If questioned later about the radio programme, it is doubtful if they would recall very much of what they heard. Other important factors include the speed at which new information is assimilated; how clearly it is presented and how much value they place on getting it right.

Lifestyle adjustments

It is doubtful that any one single event would play a significant role in making your relative's memory loss worsen but it is possible that they, like many older people, have experienced a string of life changes which have occurred in fairly close proximity. The two examples given below are used as illustrations only. You will know best what life-events have overtaken your relative and how these incidents may have affected their ability to deal with everyday affairs.

Example 1: Effects of bereavement

Changes in circumstances, however common, are not always welcomed or well planned. One example alone, that of the death of a life-partner, could set in motion a chain of distressing events. Within a short space of time an older person might become bereaved and subsequently move into sheltered accommodation, or to live closer to younger family members, and lose touch with existing friends. It is important to view the large number of losses that tend to occur for older people (for example, loss of mobility, loss of their parental/grandparent role as children become more independent, and loss of work status) as part of a larger, global picture within their lives, often termed by professional people as 'bereavement overload'. The ensuing sadness is likely to dominate thoughts and actions and cause their mental acuity to become less sharp. Losing a spouse means they have lost the main person with whom they could share past experiences and memories, so important areas of their life are no longer discussed. It is known that information, rarely used, gradually becomes forgotten or distorted and, while older people tend to remember things that have happened in the distant past rather better than recent times, these memories still need to be reviewed regularly. Often younger family members do not have the time or inclination to listen to stories being retold repeatedly by an older relative, so opportunities for recall become even less.

14

Example 2: Changes in accommodation

Older people who move away from a home where they have lived for many years, perhaps to move to a smaller home or into long term care face, in a short space of time, an overload of new information. Imagine their stress at having to meet new neighbours or numerous staff and other residents; at having to find their way around an unfamiliar building; along strange corridors, taking extra care on new stairs, learning how to work a lift or use different types of equipment such as door locks and bathroom fittings. Add to this their fears about fitting into a new culture, remembering new rules, making new friends, finding new shops or a different place to worship, and generally dealing with the politics and ethos of a strange place. It is little wonder that their memory is placed under a strain.

Focusing on the risk factors

Now that you are more aware of some of the reasons why memory loss is exacerbated in older people it might be a useful exercise to check the summary list below and note the main risk factors that might lie at the heart of your relative's memory problem. It is unlikely that there is a single cause. Some of the aggravating factors are not within anyone's control but, for others, you (and your relative) might be able to take avoiding action:

- ageing process (inevitable);
- a negative attitude towards memory function;
- anxiety or depression;
- chronic pain;
- loneliness and lack of interaction with other people;
- stressful surroundings, such a high level of background noise or an unfamiliar environment;
- poor health, exacerbated by inferior diet and lack of exercise;
- too much alcohol consumption;
- side effects of medication;
- recent bereavement with all the accompanying losses associated with this stressful period;

- memory loss brought on by a stroke (some improvements often occur with time);
- tiredness due to poor sleep patterns;
- impaired senses, for example poor hearing or sight;
- metabolic or hormonal disorders, for example an under-active thyroid gland;
- effects of long term smoking (chemicals in tobacco cause thickening of the blood and narrowing of the vessels with increased risk of clotting and blockage, the ensuing reduction in oxygen and blood to the brain leads to a form of vascular dementia);
- effects of long term sports-related head injury (eg repeated blows to the head received in boxing).

Levels of memory loss

There is some dispute within the medical profession about whether any differentiation can or should be made between varying levels of memory loss. On the one hand a number of doctors believe that some degree of age-associated memory loss is inevitable, that it should not be thought of as a separate condition. This school of thought argues that there is a continuous spectrum, ranging from mild deterioration at one end through to severe dementia at the extreme. Other doctors, however, hold another opinion. They suggest that the layers of memory deterioration are separate cognitive (perceptive) states and in their investigations have tried to distinguish differing and distinct conditions, claiming that benign memory impairment is a separate state to profound dementia.

The levels described below do not subscribe to these arguments, either way. Neither are the terms used defined medical states, they are merely descriptive aids to help relatives recognise whether some degree of memory loss exists and at which level they feel their relative might reside.

1 Lack of concentration Characterised by brief, transitory hesitation often exacerbated by tension or tiredness.

2 **Mild memory loss** Characterised by short term memory lapses with some difficulty in retaining and recalling new information, especially of recent events.

3 **Moderate memory loss** A more pronounced version of mild memory loss where the signs and symptoms occur with greater frequency and severity.

4 **Severe memory loss** Characterised by confusion, behavioural changes, loss of everyday skills and extreme difficulty in retaining and recalling basic information.

Minor memory lapses are best ignored, because drawing attention to shortcomings makes the person look foolish and only serves to increase anxiety. Moderate problems might cause annoyance for your relative and the family, but the situation can often be remedied by exercising patience and by using a few memory strategies to help reduce the effects. It would also be sensible to take some precautionary measures if you feel that your relative's extended memory problems could be a safety hazard. Signs of severe memory loss do require medical advice. If you are concerned about the state of your relative's memory function, it would be wise to consult with their general practitioner. Deterioration to Level 4 is very obvious and a person in this state is in need of close supervision. Chapter 2 gives a short memory test, which you can do in a few minutes to help assess the severity.

People who suffer from health problems often find it helpful if they can measure themselves against the rest of the population. True figures for simple age-associated memory loss are not readily available, because few studies have investigated this problem in isolation and the figures that are published do not necessarily compare like with like. The majority of research carried out in this field has concentrated on more serious forms of dementia. The figures in Fact Box 1 help give an overall picture.

Fact Box 1

- About 40 per cent of people aged 65 years or older have the mildest form of age-associated memory impairment (Clinical Review, *British Medical Journal*, Volume 324, 2002)

- About 10 per cent of people aged 65 years or older have mild cognitive impairment, a more severe form of memory loss (Clinical Review, *British Medical Journal*, Volume 324, 2002)

- Dementia affects one in 20 over the age of 65 years (Alzheimer's Society 2002)

- The number of people affected rises to one in five people over the age of 80 years (Alzheimer's Society 2002)

- The incidence of Alzheimer's disease doubles every five years over the age of 60 years (Alzheimer's Research Trust)

The good news about ageing and memory loss

This chapter might seem to have covered the more negative aspects of memory function; however it isn't all bad news. Psychologists who study memory loss have found that deterioration in the ability to remember usually occurs very slowly. Unless there is a significant cause, such as a stroke, changes in memory become noticeable over a number of years, not overnight. Take note of the following points (common to most older people) and use them to boost your relative's confidence if they appear overly concerned about their fading memory.

- It is quite normal to hold gradually less information in the temporary storage bank, for example five to six numbers instead of seven to eight, apparent when making a telephone call.
- Older people still retain the ability to remember and recall factual information well, once it is understood. Take, for example the instruction about how to work a piece of equipment – figures illustrating the rising number of older people using computers bears witness to this fact.

- Older people tend to underestimate their ability to cope (often wrongly) and subsequently shy away from participating in new situations.
- Older people still have the ability to study and remember new areas of learning, sufficiently well to pass examinations. There are several examples of octogenarians passing GCSE examinations.
- Many older people worry unnecessarily about their situation. Rather than liken their memory capacity to that of a quick-witted younger family member, encourage them to compare themselves with people of their own generation.
- Memory potential is huge and many older people have vast stores of information; little wonder then that it takes a bit longer to sort out the process. This is a fact, not a disadvantage.
- Most older people cope extremely well with moderate degrees of memory loss and usually find other ways to compensate. Some tricks and strategies to increase memory function will be explained in later chapters.

For more information

ⓘ The British Medical Association *Family Doctor Guide to Forgetfulness and Dementia*, by Dr Christopher N Martyn and Dr Catharine R Gale, published by Dorling Kindersley is available through most bookshops.

ⓘ *Remembering Well: How memory works and what to do when it doesn't*, by Delys Sargeant and Anne Unkenstein, published by Allen & Unwin.

ⓘ *Thanks for the Memory: Your guide to memory and how it works*, by Susan Aldridge, published by the Alzheimer's Society.

Conclusion

This chapter has served as an introduction to memory loss. For some carers, this might be the first time your relative has needed extra care, it may also be your first attempt at finding out more about a health problem;

for other carers, whose relative's problem is becoming more severe, reading this book may be an attempt to learn something new – about the condition or about how best to offer support.

The book has been written especially for carers and the information, advice and guidance is directed at their way of thinking. If you think it might also help your relative to deal with their memory lapses better, then share the book with them or read out parts that you feel are applicable. If the information helps with their understanding it doesn't matter who the book is aimed at!

The next chapter will tell you more about how memory loss is diagnosed and treated and who provides professional care.

2 Diagnosing memory dysfunction

Chapter 1 gave background information about the type of memory loss found more commonly in older people, to help carers understand the effects of an ageing memory. The various sections described normal memory function, including normal age-related deterioration, examples of some of the things that can go wrong and how external factors can worsen the condition. In addition, the common risk factors were listed (some inevitable and others that might be treatable) together with a brief description of different levels of memory loss to help you judge the severity of your relative's problem. Finally, some statistical facts were included to help put the problem into context. As you read the following chapters, you may wish to refer back to Chapter 1 to re-read sections that will help clarify more complex information.

Chapter 2 focuses on how a diagnosis is made and how the severity of the condition is assessed. A basic questionnaire is included to help you appraise your relative's memory performance, perhaps before seeking further advice. The test can be done quickly and should not cause undue distress. The chapter also introduces you to some of the professional people whom you might meet during the course of investigation, diagnosis and treatment, should that route be necessary.

If you are concerned about your relative's decreasing ability to remember, it would be wise to seek medical advice from their general practitioner initially. Action taken at an early stage may reassure you that their level of loss falls within expected 'normal' limits for their age group, or indicate that further tests are required. In either case, intervention has probably now alerted you to the need for greater awareness concerning their behaviour and safety. You might find that, with better supervision, the situation improves considerably. It is also possible that symptoms are being exacerbated by other physical or mental health problems that are easily treatable.

Ruling out dementia

It is possible that in your apprehensive state the words 'senile dementia' (see note below) or Alzheimer's disease are hovering in your mind. The symptoms are similar, especially at a very early stage, when these illnesses cannot be diagnosed easily. Your relative's general practitioner will explain the differences and if the doctor believes the level of memory loss your relative is displaying exceeds that which could be expected at their age, he or she can advise you about what signs to look for, should their health continue to deteriorate. For your information, the main symptoms of dementia include:

■ **Severe memory problems,** particularly for recent activities, although the ability to recall events that took place in the distant past remain unaffected until the illness is more advanced.
■ **Difficulties in communication,** where fluent speech is hampered by an inability to retrieve the correct word from their memory. As the problem progresses the person becomes less coherent, sentences are left unfinished and they may not be able to write down even a simple telephone message.
■ **Disorientation,** where the person cannot place themselves at the correct 'moment in time', ie sufferers cannot name the day of the week or the time of the year. Severe problems can occur when day and night become confused and sleep patterns get out of line.

- **Changes in usual behaviour,** which becomes more common as the condition progresses, although not everyone with dementia is affected by this trait.
- **Alteration in personality,** with certain features becoming much more pronounced; for example, some people become socially withdrawn and others experience noticeable mood swings.
- **Poor concentration,** leading to loss of practical skills, as the person finds it increasingly difficult to focus on the task in hand; for example, they might no longer be able to prepare a basic meal.
- **Falling standards** where they lose their ability to dress themselves adequately or take care of personal cleanliness – and no longer realise that this is so.

Dr Stuart, Consultant Geriatrician

'I feel that those families who do become concerned about approaching early dementia should seek advice, because drugs can now be useful to at least delay the process.'

Note on terminology

The medical profession rarely uses the prefix 'senile' when describing the condition, especially when dealing with a lay audience; nowadays the preferred term is simply 'dementia'. You may come across other terms used by professional people to describe memory loss; for example, 'age-associated memory impairment' was a description adopted in the United States (now largely superseded by 'age-associated cognitive decline'), whilst in Europe another common term was 'benign senile memory forgetfulness'.

You may also feel uncomfortable if you hear your relative being described by health professionals and in literature as having deteriorating 'mental health'; however, that is the medical language that is most likely to be used if their memory function continues to worsen and they require more substantial forms of care. The term is unlikely to be used in a derogatory sense intentionally by professional workers. The name 'dementia' might also be used by some people to explain any health state which incorporates memory loss, but in many cases it is an expression which is used loosely to describe a number of conditions affecting older people, often in the absence of any other suitable word.

Signs and symptoms of memory loss

Boxes 1 and 2 below can be used as checklists to help you decide whether the vague symptoms you are witnessing are sufficiently troublesome for you to seek advice. The examples provided are intended as guides only; they are not definitive lists covering all memory-related behaviour or everything an older person might forget to do. Use them to make some notes prior to speaking with your relative's doctor. Memory testing is an important aid in the diagnosis and differential assessment of this type of problem. The basic test provides a simple means to determine whether more formal mental appraisal is necessary. A GP or practice nurse can easily perform the test similar to Box 3 below (or a longer version) as part of a routine health check. This particular mini-memory test is well recognised and used comprehensively by GPs and geriatricians, so if you try it out at home first you can use your observations to support your case and any professional person you speak to will be talking the same language.

Dr Stuart, Consultant Geriatrician

'Doctors always advise relatives to be open and honest when they attempt to get a measure of memory impairment. Asking strange questions out of the blue without prior explanation could increase the older person's anxiety. They might also wonder about your memory state and be amazed that you don't know the answers to such basic questions yourself! In the majority of cases the fact that you are being sympathetic is likely to ease their fears.'

If you feel that a visit to the doctor is probable, it would be sensible to introduce this potential outcome from an early stage and gradually build on the idea. The NHS observes a strict code of confidentiality towards individual patients so, unless or until your relative is unable to make decisions on their own behalf, it is unlikely that you could consult with their GP officially without their knowledge and consent.

Box 1 Forgetfulness

Examples of general tasks your relative might have trouble with, resulting in the following problems:

- Failure to perform simple, everyday jobs such as buying sufficient groceries or collecting their pension

- Forgetting routine (but important) responsibilities, such as locking the door at night

- Continually re-checking recent actions, for example, whether the bed has been made

- Getting to the shops but forgetting to purchase key items

- Missing appointments

- Forgetting to take regular medication

- Forgetting names, particularly of people and places

- Misplacing objects – such as spectacles or a newspaper – around the house

- Leaving personal belongings behind at venues outside the home

- More seriously, putting themselves at risk by failing to turn off equipment such as gas, taps or electrical appliances before going to bed or leaving the house.

Box 2 Conduct

Examples of behavioural signs your relative might display:

- Telling the same stories over and over again, especially events from their earlier life

- Repeating themselves several times in a short space of time, for example, by telling you about an article they have read in the newspaper

- Worrying about lost items such as important documents, and then spending time rummaging through cupboards

- Taking longer to do basic activities, such as mental arithmetic or writing a letter

- Taking longer to learn new information or being disinclined to do so because it's too much bother

- Distrusting their memory and writing lots of information down in order to tell you at a later stage

- Telescoping time so that things that have happened a long time ago, with many years between events, become rolled together into one experience

- Mixing fantasy with reality, for example, by telling you that a set of circumstances occurred in a certain way when it is obvious that some of their tale is due to their imagination

- Believing that they have told you about something (and arguing their case!) when you know that they have not done so.

Box 3 Mini Mental Memory Test

The health professions will ask your relative questions about:

1 Their age

2 The time (to nearest hour)

3 An address (not their own) for recall at the end of the test (this should be repeated by the patient to ensure that it has been heard correctly)

4 The current year

5 The name of a familiar place

6 If they recognise two well known people

7 Their date of birth

8 The year First World War commenced

9 The name of the present Monarch or Prime Minister

10 How to count backwards from 20

Score

Each question scores one mark. Scores below seven indicate the possibility of memory impairment.

Investigating the problem

There are a number of professional people who might become involved in diagnosing and dealing with the problem. This section opens with a look at whom you and your relative might meet along the way, depending on the severity of the case. The main professional people working to diagnose and treat any form of mental health problem related to memory loss are listed here.

General practitioner (GP). Community doctor based at the local health centre or surgery. You might also hear your GP being called a Primary Health Care Practitioner. The GP is the key figure that your relative should visit first and, depending on the severity of the problem, they are able to deal with most aspects of general illnesses – from diagnosis to treatment. The majority of care given by GPs is arranged through the local surgery.

Consultant geriatrician A medically trained doctor who specialises in the treatment of older people. Specialists in geriatric medicine are based at district hospitals and they (or one of their team) see patients initially at an outpatients' clinic. The GP will make the appointment for your relative.

Psycho-geriatrician A psychiatrist who concentrates on working with older people with mental health problems; for example, severe depression. Nowadays most health trusts provide this type of specialised, 'expert' care. This role is usually hospital-based; however, the specialist will work closely with the community-based Primary Health Care team treating your relative, and might see your relative in a community setting.

Registered Mental Nurse (RMN) A trained nurse who specialises in caring for people with mental illness. RMNs work in hospital and community settings; the latter often based at a GP surgery or similar venue. A RMN (sometimes called community psychiatric nurse or CPN), should they become involved, would work closely with the GP (and psychiatrist) and would visit your relative at home.

Counsellor A therapist who is trained to listen to someone in an unbiased way and help them make decisions and take practical steps towards recovery or acceptance of the situation. Counselling for memory loss is unlikely to be offered as part of NHS care but it can sometimes be accessed through private practice.

It is natural to feel apprehensive, but doctors and nurses will try to put you at ease and the sort of questions that are likely to be asked will explore obvious points rather than be deeply searching. In preparation for the appointment, it may help if you write a brief account of how things have been. Short notes will do and you can refer to these at the meeting if you feel nervous. Always mention the most important problem or symptoms first rather than coming to the crux of the matter from an oblique angle.

How a diagnosis is made

Although each person presenting with memory loss is different, many cases share similar signs and symptoms. When your relative attends the surgery their GP will be looking for certain pointers that make up an 'early warning' check list. Depending on the information that you and your relative first offer, the doctor will wish to know in detail about recent behaviour, with discernible evidence of memory loss and significant factual examples similar to those outlined in the boxes on pages 25–26. The main objective for the doctor is to build up a complete history which, coupled with test results, helps to form a diagnosis. Your story is an essential part of the overall picture.

Joseph, a GP

'Time is a useful and inexpensive test! Observations made over time by relatives are invaluable.'

It is probable that your relative's doctor will make an unconfirmed diagnosis following the initial examination. You might then be asked to return to the surgery for further tests and/or, if the warning symptoms indicate a more serious problem, your relative might be referred to an outpatients' clinic for clinical investigations. In isolation, none of the symptoms listed on pages 25–26 indicate severe memory loss or impending dementia, and each could be caused by other problems that need investigating.

Health picture

Be prepared to give information about any of the following aspects of your relative's lifestyle and medical background to help the health professionals you meet form a complete picture.

- Family history, particularly whether other relatives in the recent past had similar problems.
- Broader health and lifestyle details, such as sleeping patterns, weight gain, headaches and any long term causes of pain.
- Details of recent medication, including drugs bought from a pharmacy, which have not been prescribed by a medical practitioner (occasionally inaccurate or conflicting dosages can give rise to symptoms resembling confusion).
- Whether (as relatives) you are aware of any contributing circumstances, such as changes in circumstances, increase in alcohol consumption, signs of depression.
- Mental acuity, perhaps by asking questions similar to those in the questionnaire above, designed to assess memory performance.

Diagnostic tests

The range of physical tests outlined below is comprehensive so it is unlikely they would all apply to your relative. Their main purpose is to signal or rule out other causes: for example, illnesses caused by an infection, vascular disorders such as minor strokes, brain tumours (often benign in nature) and diseases caused by a hormone imbalance, such as an under-active thyroid gland.

Blood checks

Blood testing is a routine start to many medical investigations, as samples of blood can be taken and checked easily in a laboratory. In isolation, looking at blood rarely provides an outright answer, but it will indicate whether or not some system within the body is malfunctioning.

- **Full blood count** The number of cells present provides vital information. For example, reduced red cells would show that a person is anaemic, while increased white cells indicate they are trying to fight an infection and a higher number of platelets means the body is trying to control bleeding. A full blood count can also give the doctor a clue to certain conditions, such as vitamin deficiency or a risk to health from alcohol abuse.

- **Blood glucose level** This test checks for the presence of age-related diabetes.
- **Electrolyte measure** This test examines the level of certain salts in the body (in particular sodium and potassium); an imbalance develops swiftly when the body is unwell.
- **Hormone levels** As a specific example relating to memory loss, a check would be made on the chemicals linked to the thyroid gland. If the blood test showed there were abnormalities further thyroid function tests might be suggested. A range of hormone tests is available.

X-rays

If other tests and symptoms indicated that an infection was present the doctor might ask for a chest x-ray to look at the lungs and heart. This would not be undertaken routinely without clear signs of a problem in that area.

Brain scans

Several versions are open to the doctor to aid investigations:

- **Computed tomography (CT)** This is a special x-ray technique that enables focused images of the brain to be taken in very small slices, half to one centimetre apart. Scans can check whether there are any underlying degenerative changes to the brain or vascular (blood) system. The resulting picture (a tomograph) can be viewed on a computer screen as a series of cross sections of the organ being examined. Any abnormal sections of brain will be clearly visible and a printout of the picture can be made if necessary
- **Magnetic Resonance Imaging (MRI)** Another technique that uses computers combined with powerful energy waves to produce a picture of the shape and structure of a body area. In this procedure radio waves (instead of x-rays) are intermittently beamed at the prescribed area. Pictures of the tissue being investigated can be viewed via a screen in a similar way to CT. The MRI technique is very useful in neurological examinations.

- **Positron Emission Tomography (PET)** This technique is currently being used in research on the brain. It allows scientists to view areas of the brain, involved with various forms of memory function, whilst the memory is in action. The work will undoubtedly be very useful in future diagnoses.

Physical examination

Investigations might include the following:

- **Blood pressure (BP) measurement** This is particularly important, as a raised BP (hypertension) can cause minute and undetected leakage of blood into the brain causing very minor strokes.
- **Neurological checks** These include tests on reflexes and optical (eye) examination. The eye is a good window into possible brain and circulatory problems.
- **Liver and kidney function tests** The liver is responsible for converting broken-down foodstuffs essential for other body action, so these tests help look for any changes in the metabolic process. Abnormal levels of protein and other enzymes might indicate that the liver is not working efficiently.

Many medical tests take several days to complete so do not be concerned if you have a lengthy wait for results.

Recognising anxiety and depression

A distressed state of mind can be a major contributing factor towards memory loss and the two predicaments are often interactive, creating a circle of fear and doubt. Imagine the situation where existing (natural) memory loss has induced mild anxiety – the person then becomes distressed and agitated causing a low-key problem to spiral into a deeper anxiety state. Their accompanying perplexity and alarm about coping makes them even more distracted – which in turn reduces their ability to concentrate on what's happening around them – and so the anxiety loop continues.

It is recognised that anxiety and depression are linked. Their character-istics are very akin to each other with symptoms occurring simultaneously. It is possible that your relative feels over-anxious and depressed at the same time, making it harder to tell the illnesses apart or be sure which feelings came first. Equally, either state can also exist separately – however, in your relative's case it doesn't really matter. If there is a problem, both conditions can be treated. The list in Box 4 below offers some clues to how the illnesses can be recognised and distinguished and, if you are worried about your relative's mental state, the examples will help you to describe their behaviour.

Grace, a GP

'Do not attempt self diagnosis or home treatment without your relative being properly assessed by a professional person; thereafter you can both follow ortho-dox and self-help approaches advised by a medical person as they often complement each other. I would support the use of both types of treatment.'

Box 4 Distinguishing between anxiety and depression

■ Anxious people feel very emotional while depressed people feel empty of emotions

■ Anxious people often speed up their thought processes and actions, leading to feelings of panic, while in depressed people these functions slow down

■ Anxiety causes tense body actions – depressed bodies often look slumped

■ Anxious people tend to seek external causes for their problems whilst depressed people are more inclined towards self-blame, guilt and unwor-thiness

■ Anxious people have deep concerns about the future but life never seems as hopeless as the feelings expressed in depression

Memory clinics

Memory clinics have been in action in the UK for over 30 years, primarily as centres where research linked to Alzheimer's disease is carried out. Most clinics require a letter from a GP before patients can be seen for assessment and diagnosis, although some private clinics will take patients direct. Many clinics prefer a GP referral as it helps to eliminate the numbers of 'worried well' people – the patients who complain of memory problems but when tested show no clinical evidence of cognitive failure. Specialist memory clinics are not available in every health district in the UK and some operate a variable age limit (eg between 50–75 years).

The procedures are similar at most clinics, involving a common set of tests and investigations. A comprehensive test, called the 'Mini-Mental Status Examination', is used by doctors for deeper investigation. It is similar to the 'memory' test in Box 3 on page 26, but is longer and it is designed to probe certain aspects of memory dysfunction more thoroughly. Your relative is likely to be asked a series of questions drawn from the following categories:

- **Orientation** Naming dates and places.
- **Registration** Repeating list of named objects (at least three) several times to record to memory.
- **Attention** Subtracting numbers or spelling words backwards.
- **Recall** Remembering the names of the objects learned earlier.
- **Language** Naming items; repeating words; following a three-stage verbal command; reading and following written instructions and writing a sentence that is sensible.
- **Copying** For example, the patient may be asked to copy a drawing of intersecting pentagons.

Note Allowances might be made in the final score based on certain aspects of the patient's background; for example, if English is not their first language.

If you accompany your relative to the clinic there are many ways that you will be able to assist. But here is a note of caution – if you are present when a health professional asks your relative questions designed to test their memory function, however much you might wish to join in, do resist the temptation to help them out. Keeping 'buttoned up' may feel difficult, especially if you have become accustomed to supplying the answer in recent times or if your relative looks to you for support, but at that moment a contribution from you would not be welcomed.

Memory clinics diagnose a wide range of memory-related conditions ranging from mild, cognitive impairment to Alzheimer-type or stroke-related dementias, depression and anxiety disorders. Clinics around the UK report a varying incidence of dementia-related memory loss, from 15–98 per cent. The figures do appear to differ widely from clinic to clinic but there are reasons for this. Some GPs test their patients more fully than others and only send patients to a centre following a fairly accurate, surgery-based diagnosis of dementia, while others do basic checks only at the surgery or health centre and send suspected cases to the clinic to be diagnosed for any type of memory loss. Don't be worried by any references to 'dementia', as being referred to a memory clinic does not necessarily indicate that your relative's GP suspects that this more serious illness is developing. All patients who attend a memory clinic benefit from more intensive investigations, appropriate support and a possible opportunity to take part in drug trials.

Dr Stuart, Consultant Geriatrician

'If a diagnosis of developing dementia is made, carers and relatives are given much help and support. I tell relatives and my patients that dementia is a disease, NOT a disgrace.'

Can memory loss be treated?

Here, it is important to be realistic about treatments and what they can achieve. It would be wrong to give the impression that age-related memory loss can be cured; however, fading function can be improved, with very positive results. Chapter 1 indicated that poor memory function can be provoked by a number of contributing factors, so it makes sense to examine your relative's personal situation, deal with some of the underlying causes and, where possible, make adjustments. In essence, any 'treatments' for memory loss can be looked at from two perspectives – the medical route and the self-help approach. For age-related memory loss, unless there is a treatable medical illness, the latter method is likely to be the most useful. With your support, your relative can be helped to regain some of their lost confidence and continue to take a hand in managing their everyday affairs.

Medical involvement

Medical intervention works mainly through the use of defined treatments and technical aids – for some illnesses and physical disabilities. But not all disorders are treatable.

Many benefits can be achieved, for example:

- taking daily medication might help prevent further strokes;
- deficiencies caused by diseases such as an under-active thyroid gland, or anaemia, or poor absorption of vitamins, can all be corrected;
- using anti-depressant therapy can bolster the debilitating effects of depression;
- pain control measures will reduce the discomfort of chronic pain, brought on by diseases such as age-related arthritis;
- dealing with impaired senses, such as poor hearing or vision, improves the quality of important 'input' skills to the brain;
- conversely, stopping unnecessary drug use or reducing dose levels might reduce drowsiness.

The use of prescribed drugs, or any other orthodox treatments and practical aids, should they be required, can only be given by the appropriate practitioner, for example, your relative's GP or an ophthalmic optician. Your foremost role here, if your relative is reluctant to seek help, might be to persuade them to visit a professional person in the first place.

Self-help approaches

The mainstay of advice described in the following chapters focuses on the self-help principle. If your relative responds well to the level of help and support that you can offer, then many basic remedies work well. If you are unsure about how much to expect, or fear that you might make matters worse, bear the following points in mind:

■ whatever you and your relative try out, if it doesn't seem to be working, stop;
■ try one thing at a time in order to avoid confusion – there is no rush;
■ don't pile on the pressure, with too high expectations, as this will cause distress and probably make the situation deteriorate;
■ it is generally accepted that a bit of self-help, practised sensibly within well-recognised and safe parameters, rarely does any harm.

Conclusion

This chapter has given basic information about how you set about getting help for your relative's memory problems and how the condition might be diagnosed. As the main carer, you may be the person who starts this process and who accompanies your relative to the various appointments. You are probably also the person who will be expected to deal with the outcomes and any advice about care, so it is important that you also understand what is happening. Most people in this situation feel apprehensive – you are not alone if you find this whole business daunting. Remember that it is all right to ask questions about any aspect of your relative's memory-state or care that you are not sure about. Try to remain positive (and realistic) as a resolute manner brings strength to your own attitude and outlook.

The next chapter looks at some of the practical issues that you can address within their personal life, with a range of hints and strategies.

3 Strategies and practical support to boost memory

Chapter 3 looks at ways in which you and your relative can work together to improve their personal circumstances, using a combination of professional treatments and self-help routines. Chapter 1 indicated that poor memory function can be exacerbated by a number of provoking factors, so it makes sense to examine your relative's personal situation, deal with some of the underlying causes and, where possible, make adjustments. Here you will find some suggestions about how to:

- introduce changes and practical aids that can help improve memory skills;

- support a person after a bereavement;

- help reduce the effects of anxiety and depression.

It is important to accept that in the majority of cases simple, age-related memory loss, as described in this book, cannot be reversed. Rather than hope for a cure, be realistic about what your relative can achieve and employ any strategy that seems to work – bearing in mind you each have differing needs. The aim is to support and guide your relative towards making the best use of their existing capacity, without over-stretching either their or your ability to cope. If they can regain some lost confidence and continue to maintain reasonable control over their everyday affairs you will have realised this aim. On good days, you might accomplish a great deal. On days that are less good, you will experience inevitable setbacks where fulfilling even the most basic tasks may be a test of your patience! However, being patient often pays off because listening to the same story three times over one cup of tea, or locating a mislaid item, could be the key that clears their mind sufficiently to concentrate on the job in hand.

Increasing mental stimulation

Authorities on memory function suggest there are four main qualities that are instrumental in developing memory power, the key techniques that are most likely to 'do the trick'. There is nothing startling in their concept, nor should they be difficult for you or your relative to master. However, there is no guarantee either that stimulating their ability to remember will have real long term advantages.

The suggested areas to work on are:

- **Attention** It is possible that many memory failures occur because your relative does not pay sufficient attention to the information being presented. For example, when they are being spoken to, or they are being introduced to a new acquaintance, their mind might already become distracted because they are thinking about their next move – what they will say in reply or how they will greet the new person – and they *fail to register* what they are being told.
- **Interest** The brain receives new material but swiftly dismisses it as boring or irrelevant if it does not catch the interest of the receiver. Perhaps your relative is doing this because they think they have 'heard it all before' or you are fussing unnecessarily, and consequently they *fail to register* new facts.
- **Organisation** Memory operates better if new information is connected to existing material, already stored. For example, when *storing* the name of a new acquaintance, the addition of a marker, that has some relevance, will help to trace that person's details in the future (see 'mnemonics', pages 43–44).

- **Practice** Practice may not bring 'perfection' in this instance, but it does help. Repeating new information a few times (especially names) and chatting over the details with another person, allows key words to become familiar. This makes them stick in the mind so that *storage* and future *recall* is easier.

Hints and rituals to help register, store and recall information

Absorbing information

Shona, carer

'I lived the closest (in our family) to an elderly aunt so I dropped by regularly to do her shopping. I soon discovered that I needed to time my visits carefully otherwise she lost interest in telling me about her shopping list. I think I interrupted the early evening news on TV once too often and got a muddled response.'

The speed and clarity at which information is presented is vital in helping older people take in new facts. When you approach a situation, try thinking in advance about what you would like to achieve and thus help your relative make best use of the way their memory works. There are many tricks that you can employ to improve their ability to register, store and recall information.

- People do differ in the times of the day that they are mentally alert so choose carefully the best moment to hold a discussion; for example, don't visit in the early morning or late at night when your relative might be drowsy.
- Try to ensure their full concentration because watching their favourite television programme and listening to you is unlikely to be a good mix. However, you must also respect their right (and desire) to some privacy, so don't breeze in and turn off the television because you have something to say.

- Try to cut out background distractions, especially if your relative is living in sheltered accommodation with lots of surrounding activity from staff and residents. Suggest that you return to their room before starting to talk about serious business.
- Emphasise the value of the information you are bringing so that they are keen to understand what you are saying.
- Show patience by allowing them time to think about what you have said and ask you any questions, without their feeling pressured.
- Get them to repeat your message so you both agree on its content.
- Don't patronise, or use demeaning language, or make belittling references to their difficulties (or age), as this is likely to cause resentment and a 'closed mind'.
- Break large chunks of detail down into manageable-sized slots over a few sessions so they don't feel overwhelmed. Prioritise the material beforehand and deliver it in a logical order.
- Reassure them that it is OK to admit to some memory loss; for example, they could say 'My memory lets me down, please could you remind me of …'

Recording and exchanging information

Frances, carer

'My mother finds that if she has forgotten why she came into a room, if she retraces her steps to the previous room and repeats her actions, it often triggers her memory about what she intended to do next. I think this trick works for most people.'

Knowing that you or your relative can rely on certain strategies will probably reduce the pressure of having to remember. Here are a number of ideas for you both to try out and, like Frances, find the ones that work best.

- Stick to well-established routines because doing things by habit is comfortable and reassuring.

- Avoid causing frustration or distress because dealing with extra emotions will slow up the person's memory process.
- If they get stuck for a word, try giving a few clues such as 'what does it sound like?' or 'which alphabet letter do you think it might start with?'
- Keep a pad and pencil (several) handy in obvious places – by the telephone, the bedside table and in the kitchen would be sensible; however, don't scatter too many about their home as scribbled messages might be left all over the place and later forgotten! Try to discourage notes written on backs of envelopes but sticky-backed 'Post-it' style notepads might work.
- Try setting up a 'day-sheet' system, using a large, firm notebook or a clipboard with pre-prepared sheets. Insert some headings such as 'date', 'message', 'problem' etc, for reminders to themselves or to you. The memory-aid can be used as a device to prompt their memory when you visit or speak on the telephone. Suggest that they get into the habit of checking the notebook at various times during the day for messages to themselves.
- Keep a shared diary system so that important dates are known by you both. For example, they might be upset if they forgot the birthday of someone special.
- If keeping a diary is too much effort, use a highlighter pen on a prominent wall calendar.
- Fit a noticeboard to the kitchen wall with a supply of drawing pins or an office-style whiteboard with coloured (non-permanent) marker pens for recording messages. Or write directly onto the door of the refrigerator.
- Attach several magnets to the fridge door for securing notes and reminders, for example, a 'things to be done today' list where items can be crossed off easily as soon as they are completed.
- Make a telephone call to speak personally or leave an answer machine message or post a notelet in an envelope (a postcard might not be private) to remind them of a forthcoming event.

Sam, carer

'I suggested to my uncle that he talked out loud to himself when doing an important task. It might sound eccentric but it was one way of concentrating his mind. I encouraged him to say loudly "I'm turning off the gas fire before I go to bed". It seemed to work and he was much less worried as he had left the fire on several times.'

Using mnemonics

Making use of 'mnemonics', the name given to the knack of linking the item to be remembered to an appropriate memory trigger, is a common and very ancient trick. The word is derived from the name of the Greek goddess of memory, Mnemosyne. The method has survived as a memory aid for many thousands of years and it is thought to have been used in the first instance by the Greek poet Simonides, in about 500BC. The key point about using mnemonics as a memory aid is that the trigger (tag), which is attached to the name, must be sufficiently significant to make the recall work. A personal system of mnemonics can be devised using several different versions, whichever feels most appropriate or comfortable for the task. Well-tried examples include:

- **The senses** Any one of the five senses – sight, smell, touch, sound, taste, can be use to create a mental link to whatever you wish to remember. Think about a job that needs to be done in the near future, then link a coloured object (sight) to the job and create a vivid picture in your mind. For example, cleaning the car could be stored as a large, yellow, soapy wash sponge. When you wish to recall the job the visual images can be brought back to the mind. People who favour this type of system often use it to store and recall lists of jobs – with each item carrying a pertinent tag.
- **Pegword system** Here a counting system is used whereby each number from 1–10 is linked to a rhyming word (see Box 5). Each time you want to remember a number-related fact, give the number a name. Many people find this system useful for memorising items such as bank card PIN numbers.

◼ **Initial letters** Word mnemonics is probably the best-known version where a sound relationship is involved. The obvious example is to re-use of the first letter of a word because it sounds the same, or has the same initial letter, as the item to be remembered. This arrangement might work well for your relative with people's names, ie the new baby great-grand daughter is 'beautiful' and she is called 'Beatrice'. Box 6 shows how you could also describe this pegword system to your relative using a phrase where capital letters form the trigger. The expression given in the illustration has been used by many generations of people to help remember the colours of the rainbow.

Box 5 Mnemonics for numbers

0	=	bow	Six	=	sticks
One	=	bun	Seven	=	heaven
Two	=	shoe	Eight	=	gate
Three	=	tree	Nine	=	wine
Four	=	door	Ten	=	hen
Five	=	hive			

Box 6 Rainbow

R	=	Red	=	Richard
O	=	Orange	=	Of
Y	=	Yellow	=	York
G	=	Green	=	Gave
B	=	Blue	=	Battle
I	=	Indigo	=	In
V	=	Violet	=	Vain

Walter, carer

'I can remember my granddad teaching me the numbering system when I was a small lad. He didn't give it a strange name but I remembered the rhyming names and numbers. I now use it with him to help trigger his memory and he hasn't forgotten the system. I have been with him at the bus stop and heard him chanting to himself "Number 87 – gate to heaven"!'

If mnemonics seem to work for your relative, you can always think up your own personal versions. The Cockney people in London have been doing this for many generations by substituting well-known and amusing rhyming slang for many common expressions eg 'up the apples and pears' for 'up the stairs'.

Making use of internal or external memory aids

Marion, carer

'My mother said that she must try to 'stretch' her brain when I suggested that she kept a notepad handy. I reminded her gently that she was quite happy to use a walking stick to support her arthritic hip joint so why not use a similar prop to help support her memory.'

Not everyone is convinced that using 'external' memory aids is the best approach, so you might need to have a few answers ready if your relative is reluctant to take this next step. Your relative might put forward the view that reliance on such strategies makes brains sluggish and no doubt they will have heard the familiar phrase 'use it or lose', implying that under-use of their brain is possibly a cause of dementia. Other people with a different opinion believe this is not the case, maintaining that the brain is not a muscle that can be stretched and extended through sheer hard work. The middle of the road argument seems to be that 'yes', it is true that continually using tricks to remember long lists will make you better at list-remembering, but in general this type of technique does not *improve* overall memory ability. The important point here, however, is that your relative is not aiming to *improve* their memory by *increasing* a special type of skill – merely to make best use of the proficiency which exists already.

At present the facts put forward by scientists seem to be:

■ keeping the brain mentally stimulated does not protect the brain against developing dementia;

■ age-related memory loss and dementia affects all categories of people from all walks of life, however good or poor their memory skills are;

■ overusing the brain by thinking or reading too much does not lead to memory problems or dementia.

At this stage of their lives, the majority of older people would wish to remain as independent as possible – and that probably means using whatever line of attack works best. External memory aids, such as notepads and reminder sheets, are relatively easy to adopt and use; families can be creative in finding the right strategy and their use should not be viewed as defeatist. This type of visible trigger is a very sensible tool when we need help in reminding us to do something practical. Internal aids, such as the mnemonics method, are less easy to adopt later in life. The technique needs to be practised and remembered, and many older people do not have the mental energy to start using a new procedure from scratch. Unless your relative is already a user of this system or keen to learn, don't impose a complex, 'mnemonic-style' approach as a general aid; instead, make use of basic versions, such as the 'sounds like' prompt, when it best suits.

Dealing with physical disability and impaired senses

Daniel, GP

'I am aware that some older people think that they are wasting my time unless they feel really poorly, but doing a health check is part of the service we offer at the health centre. The foremost role for carers here might be to persuade their relative to visit the surgery in the first place if they are reluctant to seek help, and to bring them along. Basic health checks can pick up lots of problems at an early stage.'

Chronic pain, perhaps brought on by age-related arthritis, is a clear example of a debilitating problem that can interfere with memory process: living with the discomfort of the pain; having to think about how best to remain mobile and the long-term use of pain killing tablets and anti-inflammatory drugs are some of the reasons why memory is pressured. Not making full use of existing hearing, vision and other senses can also reduce mental efficiency. In a practical way families can:

- make an appointment with their relative's GP (with their permission) to talk about any physical illness causing problems and take them along to the surgery;
- find ways to ensure they take any medication regularly and safely, as prescribed (see page 57);
- make sure their relative is warm and comfortable and takes a little exercise, to prevent arthritic joints becoming stiff in cold weather;
- deal in a sensitive manner with any side effects, such as constipation which might result from recurring use of painkillers, by suggesting a diet rich in fibre (see pages 64–68);
- remind them about the benefits of regular hearing and eye checks and take them along to their appointments;

- help them to keep ears free from a build up of earwax, perhaps by inserting oil-based remedies recommended by a pharmacist;
- ensure that spectacles and hearing aids are in good state of repair and are being used to the best effect. For example, a regular check to keep a hearing aid clean and renew the batteries can make a huge difference. There are local charities in many areas offering this service, using volunteer help; ask for contact details at the library.

Dealing with the effects of bereavement

Larry, carer

'I noticed that my father's memory for day to day matters got worse quite quickly after my mother died. She had been ill for a few years and he seemed to be the strong one but within weeks his mind seemed to fall apart. We realised that the bereavement was the main culprit and let him ponder his memories. Gradually he came out of the bad patch and started to take an interest in his garden again, but his need to recall the past became much more obvious.'

The loss of someone or something precious can have far-reaching effects for older people and in the broadest sense of the word this 'bereavement overload' means more than the death of a loved person. An older person is very likely to lose several valued things, in close proximity, perhaps triggered by the death of a spouse or partner: home, possessions, pets, good health, mental intellect, body image, power and control over their lives and so on. Some of these elements might be chosen, others will not be, either way the pain of the loss must be recognised, and support given while the person adjusts. Relatives can help by:

- Allowing emotions to be expressed eg crying, anger, fear, rather than encouraging them to 'put on a brave face for others'.
- Allowing time to grieve – within reason. It is not possible to put a time limit on grief because it cannot be measured in weeks, months or

years. You will sense if the level of grieving seems to be extending beyond its natural course.

- Encouraging their relative to keep up a regular pattern of life as sticking to a daily routine creates a sense 'habit', making it is less likely to forget obvious tasks.
- Keeping an eye on the person's health, for example, are they eating and sleeping sufficiently well.
- After an appropriate interval, encouraging an interest in new activities, and promoting these as 'a fresh start to the rest of their life – because life does move on'.
- If the grief does not seem to be easing naturally (and this does not mean banishing the loved person from their thoughts completely), it can be helpful if relatives suggest a visit to a bereavement counselling service such as CRUSE.

Paula, carer

'Since my father died I am aware that my mother has lost the main person with whom she discussed current affairs. They would listen to the news and interpret world events in their way – not always entirely accurately but it gave them something to mull over and air an opinion. They also sat together and shared the daily newspaper, with her reading out the interesting bits and my father listening. I know that she misses this interaction intensely; unfortunately, her choice of 'news' isn't always mine so I try not to switch off as she reads long spiels to me because she is expecting an answer.'

Reducing anxiety and depression

A bout of anxiety and depression in older people is often connected to an episode of bereavement so if your relative has suffered a loss, however insignificant it might appear to outsiders, if you feel they are in low spirits, it's worth monitoring the situation. Anxiety and depression can be reduced in several ways:

- By use of medication, such as taking short term tranquillisers for anxiety and longer term antidepressants.
- By dealing with some of the aggravating causes, such as sorting out financial worries or helping to reduce loneliness.
- By sharing and thus reducing the stress load, for example, it might be as simple as another person acting as their 'voice' when they have to meet with people in authority or collecting their pension if they are nervous of being robbed.
- By allowing space and time to talk through problems and then helping them to find some solutions.
- By practising complementary therapies such as aromatherapy or Bach Flower Remedies (see page 82).

For more information

ⓘ *Caring for Someone with Depression*, by Toni Battison, published by Age Concern Books.

ⓘ Cruse Bereavement Care offer counselling, support for relatives and a range of literature (see page 166).

ⓘ Counsel and Care offer a full range of services for older people and their relatives, including counselling, information and advice (see page 166).

Conclusion

This chapter has provided you with a range of strategies and practical advice to help you maintain or improve your relative's ability to cope more easily. Carers are rarely superheroes, so don't even attempt to put all of the suggested tactics into place – wherever possible go along with your relative's wishes and what you feel is within their capabilities. Expect some pitfalls and days when emotions are bit strained.

The next chapter will look at helping to manage some of the risks associated with household routines and local environment, when an older person's memory is failing.

4 Creating a safer environment

Now that you feel your relative needs additional support, it would be a sensible move to look more carefully at all areas of their life. This is an opportunity to spend time weighing up the risks to their safety, against your need for increased vigilance and possible intervention. You may feel that you have now entered another phase of the caring process and, no doubt for your relative, it will be a time for reflection, as they begin to admit (willingly or not) that they do need extra care.

This chapter will help you to:

- review household management and set up reassuring support mechanisms;

- recognise and deal with various risk elements to increase safety;

- offer support to a relative who has experienced a change in accommodation;

- make sensible adjustments to current travel arrangements.

The sections below are very comprehensive, to cover a diverse range of needs. It is OK to skip over the parts or 'ideas' lists which are not currently applicable to your relative – you may need to return to these at a later stage. The hints are presented mainly in list form to help you do a quick assessment and create a more 'user-friendly' environment.

Providing practical help around the house

Brains that are bombarded with excess information become overloaded and work more slowly, a bit like a sluggish piece of mechanical equipment. If your relative is struggling to manage their day-to-day household affairs alone, perhaps an offer from family members (or friends and neighbours if they are willing) to share some of the tasks and *subtly* to reduce their load may be very welcome. This does not mean marching in and taking over! Simple offers of help to assist with planning and practical tasks could make a huge difference. Try to remember that it's their home and if their way of doing things isn't up to modern standards or how you usually operate – so what? Does it matter? Make a few discreet changes by all means, without condemning their less-than-efficient, but time-honoured methods.

Start by reviewing how things are done at present, and build up a list of jobs which gradually become your responsibility, for example:

■ Check the larder/refrigerator together before compiling a shopping list.

■ Offer to purchase some of the bigger items on their behalf.

■ Make sure there is a reserve store of essential items – dried food, toilet rolls and the like – in obvious visual places.

■ Check 'use-by' dates on stored items and move the 'use-first' commodities into view.

■ Find ways to ensure bills are paid on time. The direct debit facility is most obvious, but not everyone has a suitable banking account or likes using such systems. Keeping a checklist of due dates yourself, and then gently probing whether the bill has arrived, is another solution.

■ Keep an eye on the mail piles anyway, as letters might get overlooked, not be opened or put to one side and the contents forgotten. A basic folder or basket near the front door could be used as a temporary storage before sorting and transferring to a more permanent home; for example, an alphabet-type storage folder with separate pockets that you set up and manage together makes a useful one-spot container. Fit a set of hooks in the hallway for hanging keys.

■ Oversee the care of pets, such as removing fleas from cats and dogs, cleaning out a birdcage, making veterinary appointments for annual checks and injections.

Larry, carer

'I am fortunate because I live within a manageable distance of my father. I am able to visit regularly so it helps me keep on top of jobs and makes discreet checking easier. I feel that by popping in and out quite often I am more likely to notice things that look different and it feels less as if visiting time is spent in snooping and asking questions.'

Finding misplaced objects

Marion, carer

'My mother is continually rummaging for envelopes and bits of paper. She had a letter yesterday and as she sat in the chair thinking about its content, she wanted to reread it – but today it's missing! This ritual might happen several times a day over some item or other. I help in the search if she is becoming too frustrated but normally I let her forage as it does pass time and there is little I can do. Usually the item is retrieved from an old handbag or a drawer.'

Losing and then feeling compelled to find misplaced articles is very common. Much of the time you probably won't be present so you will not always know about the numerous searches that take place. If your relative lives in your home you may hear the evidence of paper rustling and drawers being opened successively. Follow Marion's advice and intervene only if the search is causing distress. You cannot be responsible for every mislaid postcard.

Hints include:

- Establishing permanent homes for categories of articles, for example, a folder for recent letters or a designated drawer for financial papers.
- Discouraging the habit of pushing envelopes and other scraps of paper behind the clock or stuffed into a bookcase – or whichever spot your relative favours.
- Helping your relative to discard unwanted items at regular intervals, for example, once a week before the rubbish collection (or suggest that someone else is around if you fear that vital items may be thrown out).
- Have a more thorough clearout every six months or so to prevent too large a build-up of trivia and clutter.
- Don't push your relative into throwing out articles of sentimental value – but you can argue for some semblance of rationality when they try to keep too many newspaper cuttings.

Improving safety

Reviewing your relative's safety is a vital element of their care, which you must assume as part of your responsibilities. Sorting out this type of broader issue may feel far removed from dealing with the memory loss problem; however, you could reason that, by addressing the bigger picture, you will help your relative feel safer, which in turn removes some of the worries which might be clouding their mind. Most of the safety risks listed below fall directly within the realm of 'potential dangers', which could be aggravated by an episode of forgetfulness. The checklist is quite comprehensive and many items are not quick jobs. Use the reminders to draw up your own 'hit' list, and then prioritise the work into urgent tasks and those which can be scheduled over a longer period. Then decide whether the activity is a DIY job or one that needs the skill of a specialist tradesman. Spread the load throughout the year and set aside a few designated days.

'I say to my dad, "let's set a goal for next week, we'll have a go at the kitchen in time for your birthday". That way he sees it as a job to be done to get tidy before his birthday tea and the date sticks in my mind.'

In practical terms the work you undertake should cover those areas within your relative's house and garden where they have direct access and accountability, but don't overlook any shared spaces for which a landlord is liable. For example, an ill-lit stairwell or loose handrail is a potential hazard which might get repaired more speedily by a landlord if you make the request on your relative's behalf.

It is important to accept that you cannot foresee every potentially harmful event, neither can you turn your relative's home into a totally risk-free zone. The section below is categorised to enable you to undertake a general risk assessment; it is not a definitive checklist and neither will everything concern your relative's personal environment or situation.

Utilities

- Check the electricity supply and equipment for correct fuses, frayed cords, up-to-date wiring, safety standard marks. Don't forget such items as electric bed-blankets, which may have become very worn.
- Look at the water supply for dripping taps, well-protected water tanks, leaks from pipes or drains. Do an extra check after a spell of very cold weather.
- Inspect the gas supply and equipment (for example, boiler, fires, carbon monoxide alarms) and discuss guidelines for remembering to turn off appliances at night.

Fire safety

- Check all types of fires.
- Be aware of lax smoking habits (cigarettes, cigars, pipes). Place ashtrays around the house and discuss guidelines about smoking in bed.

- Fix an adequate number of fire alarms and renew batteries regularly.
- Provide a fire blanket or extinguisher, placed in an accessible spot.
- Provide a heavy-duty torch, situated in an obvious place, for emergency use.
- Discourage the use of matches and candles.

Kitchen and cooking

Check arrangements and equipment to reduce the risk of:

- scalds and spillage, by providing pans that are not too heavy to lift when full; try to keep all surfaces near cookers smooth and free from too much clutter and the work top adjacent to the top of the stove should be on the same level;
- burns and fire accidents, by going over guidelines for cooking with very hot temperature such as chip fat or, better still, get rid of chip/ frying pans and encourage the use of oven-ready or microwave-type food;
- illness caused by poor hygiene by making regular checks on utensils, refrigerator and cupboards.

Bedroom and bathroom

- Check furniture for stability.
- Use bed covers that are easy to fit and launder.
- Ensure water from system does not run too hot to cause a scald.
- Supply a non-slip bath mat and fit grab rails.

Security

- Check window and door locks, and fit a door chain and peep-hole. Discuss ways that will remind your relative to close easily accessible windows at night or fit internal safety screens.
- Fit a burglar alarm (if provision of a device would increase safety and peace of mind) but not if it is so complicated that your relative has to remember security code numbers or they would worry about setting it off accidentally.

- Fit a small household safe (with proviso as above).
- Arrange a safe place where a spare key is kept for emergency access, either with a close neighbour or by fixing a key safe (a secure box with a combination lock which can be purchased from a lock-smith and fitted to an external wall).

Personal safety

- Position furniture safely.
- Secure or avoid loose rugs.
- Fix hand rails at key points.
- Reduce the risk of mugging by discussing guidelines for carrying money and other valuable items.
- Check car or bicycle for safety and efficiency, for example MOT test, garaging facilities, bicycle brakes and locks.

Garden and external entrances

- Fit external lights, preferably the type which react to someone approaching.
- Check steps, pathways and patios.
- Check for safety hazards or fill in a garden pool if it's too much work to maintain.
- Go through the garden shed looking for poorly working locks, rusty equipment, chemical storage, inflammatory items, broken glass.
- Inspect fences for security breaks, including lock on rear gate.

Taking medication

Peter, carer

'I found that I needed to intervene and speak to my mother's GP when she became more forgetful and I discovered a build up of tablets. Her drug-taking habits have become erratic in recent months so my wife or I inspect the packets when we visit to see whether the tablets appear to have been taken. The GP says the odd missed dose is not vital in her case so keeping a closer eye on what she's up to is OK.'

There are several issues to take into account here to ensure that medication is taken regularly and safely. Peter and his wife live nearby so they can be vigilant but they did take advice from their relative's GP and did not make this type of decision alone. Missing doses may not be a sensible option for certain medicines. A number of suggestions are presented so choose the method that you believe will work best and give it a try. It would be very confusing for your relative if too many systems were set up at any one moment; therefore, allow time for each new strategy to become accepted practice before deciding whether or not it is working. Then you can make an informed decision about whether or not to introduce a further tactic.

- Write clear instructions about when and how tablets should be taken, especially if your relative takes multiple doses. For example, draw a day sheet in a matrix form on a sheet of paper, with times and tablets marked in square boxes, to give a clear, visual time table.

- Encourage your relative to take the tablet from the correct section of the packet, marked by days of the week – and explain why this helps to prevent misuse.

- Be sure that your relative can open the containers or packets easily. Although screw tops are used less often these days, breaking the seal on foil packaging can be fiddly also, especially if fingers are stiff and the tablets are small. The name of the day printed on the seal may also be difficult to read.

- To help with both memory and avoiding packaging difficulties you can purchase special containers (from a pharmacy) where the doses for a day or a week can be inserted into separate compartments.

- Agree a designated place in the house where tablets are kept easily visible. For example, pills for bedtime might be better kept separately from those that must be taken during the day – one supply on the bathroom shelf and others in the kitchen next to the tea caddy (provided there is no risk to young children).

- If you are not the person who collects prescribed drugs from the pharmacy, try to have a system for checking that the medicines supplied are the correct type and dosage (especially repeat prescriptions) as mistakes can occur.

Peter, carer

'Our grandchildren visit my mother's house occasionally, so we or our daughter take responsibility for organising safe storage for all the tablets away from their reaches – as a temporary measure – we then take care to return the packets to their usual places for her to find easily.'

Adjusting to changes in accommodation

If your relative has recently moved house or into a care home, whatever their reasons for moving, it is inevitable that they will experience some effects after such a major life change. As a family you will all need to make adjustments and come to terms with the new situation. In the early days you could try following some of the suggestions below:

- Speak with the manager of the home about how best to help your relative settle into an institution-type environment with its various regulations and 'traditions'.
- Speak with near (new) neighbours or other residents – either with your relative's agreement or in such a way that you do not seem to be inviting an outsider to take over.
- Be sure they can find the way to the shops easily, and are not confused by a maze of road junctions – perhaps you could both look for obvious signs that help to mark the route.
- Set up a postal re-direction service.
- Go through the instructions for any unfamiliar equipment, such as a new microwave cooker or the buttons on a television remote control panel, and let them practice a few times until they feel confident to manage alone.
- If you are visiting your relative in a care home, find a quiet corner to discuss business matters or listen to any worries, away from other residents.

Michael, who cares for his uncle

'When my uncle moved into a care home, I walked around the immediate environment with him several times until he was sure of his boundaries and could find his way back to his room. We did this in the corridors of the home and the surrounding streets, as residents were allowed to visit the shops nearby, but the neighbourhood was new to him.'

Transport and mobility

Travel may be a problem, especially if driving is restricted, if your relative does not live within easy walking distance of the shops, or because they are fearful of getting lost. If they are nervous about being out alone your relative may not want to venture far from home, even for a shopping trip. Without being alarmist there are stories of older people setting out in a car, becoming disorientated and forgetting where they have parked it or forgetting which bus number to catch home. If you and your relative feel that they are no longer able to leave the house independently, without risk, you can look out for transport schemes for older and disabled people, available in most areas, similar to those listed below:

- **Dial-a-Ride and Community Transport Schemes** These provide door to door services for shopping or similar outings for people who cannot use public transport (see page 165).
- **Hospital Car Schemes** Such schemes are usually run by the ambulance service and arranged through health centres or GPs' surgeries. They are available only for people who have a medical condition and cannot get to the hospital independently. One companion is usually allowed.
- **The Blue Badge Scheme** Formerly known as 'The Orange Badge Scheme', this provides a national arrangement of parking concessions for people with severe walking difficulties who travel as drivers or passengers. Badge holders are exempted from certain parking

restrictions – including free parking at on-street parking meters and for up to two hours on single and double yellow lines in England and Wales. Badges are issued for a three-year period through social services departments. Check local rules carefully as some London Boroughs do not offer free parking arrangements.

■ **Motability** This charity was set up to help those disabled people who want to spend the mobility component of their Disability Living Allowance or War Pensioner's Mobility Supplement on a car or wheelchair. Vehicles may be purchased or leased and help may be available with the cost of special adaptations. A relative, friend or carer may apply and drive on behalf of a disabled person (see page 171).

■ **Concessionary rail fares** All train operators accept a railcard that offers concessionary fares to older and/or disabled people, giving up to one third off a range of rail tickets. An application form and relevant information booklets called can be found at most stations or from the Disabled Persons Railcard Office (see page 168). All rail operators give extra help to older or disabled travellers, particularly if they have advance notice.

■ **Shopmobility** Shopmobility schemes provide free wheelchair or scooter loan services in many town centres for anyone with a mobility problem. Users can usually park free or be met at the bus station or taxi rank by prior arrangement. An escort service is often available for people who are visually impaired or wheelchair users.

■ **Taxicard** This and other similar services provide subsidised taxi fares. They are run by many local authorities for permanently disabled people who are unable to use public transport. One passenger may accompany the cardholder. Ask at your town hall.

■ **Tripscope** Tripscope offers a free nationwide travel and transport information and advice service for older and disabled people (see page 175). Tripscope will help with planning a journey, but it is not a travel agency so cannot make bookings.

■ **The Community Transport Association** This association has services to benefit providers of transport for people with mobility problems (see page 165).

■ **The Disability Living Allowance Unit** Part of the Department for Work and Pensions (see page 176 under 'Vehicle Excise Duty'), this unit gives information about exemption from road tax for vehicles used exclusively by or for disabled people receiving the higher rate of the mobility component of Disability Living Allowance (DLA) or War Pensioners' Mobility Supplement. DLA is not available to people who claim for the first time after the age of 65 years. You may claim on behalf of the person you look after by completing an application form from your local DWP office.

For more information

ⓘ Age Concern Factsheet 26 *Travel information for older people.*

ⓘ Contact your local authority for more information about local schemes to help with transport.

Conclusion

In a similar vein to the previous chapter you have been offered a large list of suggestions and options. Deal with those that are most important, as a priority – without causing yourself undue stress; then work your way through the others in your own good time and don't feel bad if you slow up a bit! Even carers need to pace themselves. The next chapter will look at helping to make the best of your relative's health.

5 Keeping healthy

Early chapters have offered you some practical advice to help you support your relative in various situations – personal and environmental. The success you achieve in dealing with their memory problems is likely to be more effective if their general health remains good. The tips below focus on basic health promotion ideas and guidance designed to maintain or perk up your relative's lifestyle.

In a similar way to memory enhancement, the emphasis focuses on consolidation rather than huge leaps forward in terms of improvement. There are certain areas that might show results; for example, if your relative has been feeling a bit jaded, this listlessness may improve with a more nutritionally balanced diet or by doing something about iron-deficiency anaemia or chronic constipation. If they have been sitting in a chair getting bored, then stepping up their exercise level could liven their spirit as well as their muscles. But don't increase the pressure to do anything against their natural inclination, and don't lose sight of the key aim – which is to help their memory to continue functioning as well as possible.

Diet and nutrition

Gemma, dietitian

'The word "diet" usually conjures up images of sparse portions and grumbling hunger pangs. However, in this context, the word "diet" means "what your relative eats" rather than "how they can lose weight"! It is never too late to listen to general advice about sensible eating and there are specific diets to help older people improve poor appetite and gain energy.'

Nutrition and diet are important factors in any health programme. Your relative may have become overweight or they may have been eating incorrectly – either type of eating behaviour can be affected by poor memory. Menus can be designed to build up strength or reduce calories, depending on what dietary regime is required. There are many stories around of older people living on a diet of bread, jam and tea. A review of what your relative eats could be one of the first steps you can take to help them towards a healthier lifestyle, because adjusting the diet is a relatively easy step to take.

Some people inherit a tendency to be a certain shape and others gain or lose weight more readily than the next person. In basic terms, anyone who eats more, or fewer, calories than they burn up will usually go up or down in weight. The simple rule for controlling weight is to eat foods that are energy-rich to put on weight or foods that are calorie-reduced to lose weight. When helping your relative to cut back or increase their calories, it is important to keep an eye on the nutritional content of the diet and not reduce their intake of valuable vitamins and minerals. If your relative has a 'picky' appetite, select foods that give a good value per calorie. For example, chocolate is one of the first things that overweight people avoid, but it is a useful source of iron and calories, in an easily digestible form, if your relative is eating very little.

Joan, dietitian

'The good news is that a lot of benefit can be gained by making minor changes. It is important that your relative continues to enjoy food so don't make dramatic changes overnight – introduce new foods and cooking methods gradually and buy a variety of foods so that a healthy balance is maintained.'

Eating problems

Older people stop eating properly for many reasons, not only because of poor memory. Check the list below to identify any explanation why your relative might be struggling to maintain an interest in food. For example, are they:

- too tired or listless to eat (or shop);
- unable to chew because their dentures no longer fit properly;
- uncomfortable from an over-acid stomach before or after eating;
- constipated due to the side effect of taking various medicines;
- bored by a plain, bland and repetitive diet.

Finding solutions

Maureen, practice nurse

'In this situation there is nothing wrong with the old saying "what you fancy does you good". I often quote it to my patients and their family.'

For pick-me-up tips to improve eating habits you could try the following suggestions:

- ask your relative what foods would trigger their taste-buds as small amounts of 'snack-type' food may be better than a 'proper' meal;
- provide smaller meals on a small plate to avoid the overwhelming sight of a normal-sized helping;

- let your relative eat on request, when they feel peckish – ie 'little and often';
- choose meals with interest and nutritional value, attractively presented;
- keep food light – eating stodgy, hard-to-chew food saps energy quickly;
- ensure food is moist as this will be easier to eat than dry food;
- liquidise foods into easy-to-swallow drinks using milk or fruit juice as fluid;
- keep the freezer well stocked with a choice of refreshing ice-creams;
- try all-in-one meal-drinks and use these as a drink after or instead of a meal (some makes are available on prescription);
- increase the proportion of fibre-rich/high residue foods if constipation is a problem due to the side effects of medicines, and speak to their doctor, a pharmacist or the practice nurse about whether taking gentle laxatives might be appropriate;
- avoid rich, spicy food if this causes indigestion; conversely, if your relative's sense of taste is reduced try peppering up taste-buds with strongly flavoured food;
- offer a glass of sherry as an *aperitif* (see alcohol section on page 68);
- resist hassling your relative if they lose interest in food – a relaxed, 'no-problem' atmosphere is more likely to succeed;
- offer a little help – or cut food into manageable-sized portions, or offer to feed your relative if they tire very easily;
- keep a supply of snack bars handy which can be nibbled at will.

Sian, a carer

'My aunt and I often share a quiet meal together – it's a good time for me to sit with her for a bit and catch up on family news – and I let her eat while I do most of the talking.'

Build-up diet

This way of eating is devised to help people maintain or build up their weight. It involves introducing into the diet foods that are high in energy and protein, with the emphasis on richness and increased calories. Many older people experience eating problems and everyone needs a certain level of energy to maintain their body mass, even if they are very inactive. A diet that is advised for someone who is losing weight, or to help increase weight, is designed especially for that purpose. It is not recommended as a long term regime for people who are eating well.

Choose a selection of foods regularly from the following lists when preparing meals, to help increase calories.

- **High energy foods** Bread, pasta, cereals, cake, sweet biscuits, and glucose sweets.
- **High protein foods** Meat, poultry, fish, beans, lentils, eggs, milk and cheese – but to reduce the risk of infection cook eggs well and avoid dairy products made from unpasteurised milk.
- **Rich fatty foods** Oils, butter, margarine, fatty meats and oily fish, full-fat dairy products (eg fresh cream), nuts and mayonnaise. Look for labels that state 'whole milk' and 'full-fat' rather than products that claim to be low-fat or 'light'.
- **Vitamins and minerals** While vitamins and minerals are contained in most foods, some of the best sources are raw or lightly cooked fruit and vegetables with the skins intact.

If your relative is frail and has lost weight, use subtle ways to introduce extra goodness, without adding too much bulk. For example:

- Add extra milk or cream to soups, puddings, custard, mashed potato, breakfast cereals and drinks in the form of fortified milk foods (available from pharmacies), evaporated or condensed milk or dried milk powder and use milk when the recipe states water.
- Add extra lentils, split peas, beans or egg noodles to meat stews and casseroles.
- Put a spoonful of real cream, rich ice-cream or condensed milk on to puddings.

- Use extra honey or syrup on breakfast cereals or porridge (made with milk or single cream).
- Keep a selection of nibbles, such as peanuts, crisps and dried fruits in handy dishes about the house.
- Spread butter, margarine and mayonnaise more thickly, and add to mashed potato and vegetables.

If your relative is overweight, you will need to encourage them to reduce the quantity of calories they consume by following a diet that is high in fruit and vegetables but lower in fat and carbohydrates. A practice nurse at the surgery could offer you a leaflet giving simple dietary guidelines if it would help motivate them to adjust their eating habits.

Alcohol

In general, the main message from doctors and scientists suggests that, for the majority of people, alcohol taken in small amounts may be beneficial and does no obvious harm. It is also acknowledged that for a small proportion of the population, alcohol can have unpleasant effects; for example a person who is feeling low might increase their alcohol intake in the mistaken belief that it will relieve their mood, as in the expression 'drowning your sorrows'. Some people also believe that alcohol gives courage and the energy to cope with life. Unfortunately, any relief given by alcohol soon wears off. The feeling of blues then appears worse, and the inclination is likely to be to increase alcohol consumption. In the general population, excessive drinking is strongly linked to many causes of illness and death including cancer, liver disease, strokes, and accidental death.

If your relative enjoys a drink and there is no evidence of alcohol abuse, the indications are that an occasional drink may be both pleasurable and beneficial when taken in moderation. If you have any concerns about the amount of alcohol your relative is drinking, approach the subject sensitively and (provided they are able to discuss the situation rationally) try to work out between you how you might deal with the problem. Some tips include:

- helping your relative to avoid the temptation of using alcohol as a mood booster;
- advising them to sip drinks slowly to make each glass last longer;
- avoiding undiluted spirits or drinking on an empty stomach;
- offering non-alcoholic wines or beers, and exploring the wide range of soft drinks now available;
- suggesting that they seek help if the situation is becoming a problem.

If there are signs that your relative's memory loss is affecting their judgement and their alcohol intake has become excessive, without any signs of reasonable control, the situation calls for a more radical approach otherwise they could potentially be at risk. Try to monitor their behaviour and habits. Look out for classic signs that indicate a person has drunk too much alcohol or is stockpiling large quantities of alcohol without realising they are doing so. Your immediate course of action depends on the circumstances. If they are obviously getting tipsy you could seek advice from Drinkline, the national alcohol helpline listed on page 168, or speak with their GP who might recommend a locally-based alcohol counselling service. Most organisations offer support to relatives as well as the main person.

Note Some forms of illness can mimic being intoxicated, for example, a diabetic coma, so be very careful here about what steps you take – don't just assume that your relative is inebriated.

For more information

- Alcohol Concern offers information in the form of factsheets, leaflets and a journal but not direct advice (see address on page 162).

- Drinkline National Alcohol helpline, providing confidential information, help and advice about drinking to anyone, including people worried about someone else's drinking (see address on page 168).

Smoking

Memory loss problems are unlikely to be greatly affected by any smoking habits your relative might have, although it is possible that the action of carbon monoxide, a poisonous gas also found in car exhaust fumes, might be reducing their ability to think with optimum clarity. Tests have shown that carbon monoxide in the bloodstream can reduce the amount of oxygen being transported to vital organs such as the brain by up to fifteen per cent, so a lowered oxygen-rich blood supply could mean reduced brain activity. It would be interesting to note how often they 'forget' to stock up on supplies! However, smoking might be exacerbating other health problems, such as any tendency they might have towards cardio-vascular problems, thus increasing the risks of a stroke or heart disease. It is a myth that smoking may not be harmful. The proven evidence from a large number scientific studies show that all forms of smoking (cigarettes, cigars and pipes), damage health. The facts about smoking-related illnesses make for sober reading. Smoking is the biggest avoidable cause of premature death and ill health; the earlier a person starts to smoke the greater their likelihood of developing smoking-related diseases.

Grace, a general practitioner

'It's never too late to feel the benefits of giving up, and it's one of the most effective changes that anyone can make to improve their health. However, most GPs would not encourage a patient to give up smoking if it is likely to worsen the symptoms of other mental health problems, such as depression.'

Most people do understand that smoking is bad for their health, especially if a family member has developed a tobacco-related disease. If your relative smokes, they may have been told to give up. But the problem often lies, not in the acceptance that cigarette smoke is the culprit, but in the ability to actually stop. Quitting smoking is not an easy thing to do as long-term smokers are usually addicted to nicotine and may suffer severe withdrawal symptoms. It can be particularly difficult when stress levels are increased by boredom or anxiety about the future. If your relative's desire to smoke is very strong, suggesting that they attempt to give up may not be realistic. Be ready to offer encouragement if they do wish to cut back or stop the habit.

Tips to stop smoking

- Listen to your relative and try not to criticise any lapses. Be sympathetic but firm.
- However irritable they become, don't suggest they start smoking again.
- Change routines so that old habits don't make it easy to light up. Identify times and places that make your relative particularly vulnerable to temptation, and alter behaviour if necessary. For example, suggest they sit in a different chair, drink tea instead of coffee and change routines after a meal – as all of these may be associated with a previous smoking habit.
- Offer plenty of beverages, as ex-smokers need to flush the chemicals well out of their system. Fruit juice is particularly good as vitamin C helps to rid the body of nicotine.
- Suggest different forms of entertainment to help combat boredom, particularly activities which involve using the hands.
- Offer plenty of praise and support, but don't overdo the sympathy. Some sensitive people may prefer not to be reminded. Ask your relative which approach would work best for them.
- Suggest that your relative tells people they need to give up for health reasons. That way family and friends won't smoke in their presence and, hopefully, won't tease them for their efforts.
- Talk about the benefits of giving up. For example, after a few days the sense of taste and smell begin to return; after a few weeks the lungs are cleaner and breathing becomes easier; and after a year the risk of a heart attack is reduced by 50 per cent.
- Highlight the money that is being saved, and think of ways you can use it to treat yourselves!

For more information

ⓘ Talk to other ex-smokers or telephone the freephone helpline run by an independent charity Quitline (0800 002200) that provides confidential and practical advice for people wanting to give up smoking.

ⓘ NHS Smoking Helpline 0800 169 0 169 offers similar help and support to give up all forms of smoking.

Exercise

Exercise is good news for everyone, even for people who are not particularly mobile. Whatever the level of physical activity a person undertakes, it must be tempered to suit their capabilities. Information in a book can only be written in a general way, so before you encourage your relative to take any form of exercise, they *must* check with their doctor first and be sure they understand what is suitable for them. Not all exercise need be strenuous, and no one would suggest your relative take up vigorous sports. Start gently with a mild physical activity and consider joining in yourself – shared activity is much more pleasurable than exercising in isolation.

Philip, health promotion adviser

'It is never too late to derive some benefit from exercise, the advantages are well proven. Exercise helps improve physical strength, mobility and mental well-being. It's very good for reducing stress as it boosts the hormones which produce feelings of happiness and the movement gently relaxes muscle tension. Muscles work more smoothly, with less effort, if they are made to work regularly. The Health Development Agency recommends exercise that boosts the three S's – strength, suppleness and stamina – all within moderation.'

Gina, leisure centre manager

'Ask at your local leisure centre for classes that are especially designed for older people. If none are running, speak to the manager and put in a request – it may be because no one thinks there is a need. At my centre the classes are advertised at all the GP surgeries and health centres in the area so we get lots of referrals by GPs.'

Exercising safely

Whichever activity your relative chooses, it is important to be aware of a few safety rules, even after they have their doctor's approval:

■ Start exercising gradually and build up exertion levels at a rate that feels comfortable. No-one should behave as if they are training for the Olympics.

■ Don't exercise for at least two hours after a meal as the digestive system places an automatic demand on the blood supply to digest the food.

■ Wear clothes that are loose and comfortable, and shoes or trainers that provide adequate support.

■ Never rush straight into the most strenuous part of the activity. Start and stop at a gentle pace to allow muscles to warm up and cool down before and after exercise.

■ Drink plenty of fluids, but not alcohol, as this increases dehydration.

■ Stop immediately if there are any signs of breathlessness, chest pains or feeling unwell in any way. If exercise causes problems, however minor, it would be wise to inform the doctor before continuing with the programme.

Ringing the changes

Nat, physiotherapist

'When starting to exercise after a period of inactivity, look at leisure sports to get the body moving gently. Choose activities that are pleasurable and start off cautiously because too great an effort may reduce enthusiasm. Muscles that have not been exercised need to stretch gently so "start and finish slowly" is the simple rule that can be applied to all the examples listed below.'

The following activities are classed as leisure hobbies rather than exercises for fitness fanatics; some can be done alone, some need a partner. If your relative would like to join a club, look in the local Yellow Pages or ask for details at the public library.

- **Walking** This is a good choice if you have both been inactive as it boosts stamina and allows fitness to build up at a steady rate. Walking needs no special equipment, it is free, relaxing and pleasurable if shared with a companion. If your relative has become very debilitated by inactivity they must start very gently, perhaps with regular short walks, gradually increasing the pace and distance over a few weeks. If you have any concerns about them getting lost, or the area where they live is not suitable, discourage walking out alone.
- **Swimming** Another good exercise for people of all ages, swimming combines the three S's – stamina, strength and suppleness. It is often described as the ideal activity and can be a great stress reducer. Swimming is especially good for people who are overweight or have joint or back problems as the water supports the body. If your relative expresses doubts about donning a costume in public tell them that the water offers a good camouflage and, if somebody gets a laugh at their expense, it will do them good!
- **Gardening** This is a wonderfully relaxing way to combine exercise with fresh air and do lots of bending and stretching. Recent research into horticultural therapy has shown it to be very beneficial for people feeling a bit low.

- **Bowling** Your relative might like to join a club to get the best advantage from indoor and grass bowls and try the ten-pin variety with younger family members for some challenging play. All forms of bowling are excellent for suppleness and relaxation.
- **Exercise and dance classes** These are readily available in most areas. Ask at a leisure centre about classes to suit your relative's age and ability level. Both types of exercise are good for stamina, strength and suppleness.

Sian, a carer

'My aunt joined the Tea Dance Club at the local day centre. She looked forward so much to the weekly outing and found that she could remember the steps to most of the 'Old Tyme' dances that were on the programme. Music and movement go well together and the combination is especially relaxing and enjoyable.'

Leg cramps

Even small increases in exercise may cause leg cramps for some people, particularly if it is after a long period of inactivity. Your relative's doctor will advise about taking exercise if leg cramps are painful.

For more information

ⓘ For details of a local adult sport and leisure activity classes contact the Community Education department at your local education authority, or private leisure centres.

ⓘ The Sports Council provides general information about all sports (see page 174).

ⓘ EXTEND provides recreational movement to music for older and less able people. EXTEND is active in many parts of the UK and trained teachers provide one-to-one sessions for those who require specialised exercise (see page 169).

Sleeping well

Tension and stress are at the heart of many sleep problems, causing early waking or difficulty dropping off as thoughts race around the brain. If worry is making you or your relative sleep badly, don't rush for medication. Instead, try practising a few of the tips given below. You also need to be aware that older people naturally take longer to fall asleep, are more likely to wake during the night and tend to wake earlier in the morning. However, if sleep disturbance continues to be a problem, do encourage your relative to discuss this with their doctor.

Tips to help settle at night

The following suggestions may be helpful:

- go to bed at a regular time, with a regular routine;
- make everything as cosy as possible, with a warm room and comfortable bed;
- don't eat a rich, heavy meal late in the day;
- avoid stimulating drinks that contain alcohol or caffeine later in the day and choose a milky drink at bedtime;
- cut back on evening fluids if a full bladder is the cause of waking;
- read or listen to the radio until the mind feels naturally sleepy;
- if waking in the night is a problem do something to break the fidgety mood – rather than lie tossing and turning, get up and watch some television and repeat the milky drink with a biscuit;
- take regular exercise to tire the body, but not too late in the day as strenuous exercise releases hormones that are stimulating;
- rest and cat-nap during the day but resist having too long a sleep as this simply reduces the amount needed at night.

Relieving boredom

Kathy, carer

'Dick, my husband, was used to being busy so he did find it strange to have no energy and poor concentration after a series of small strokes. I bought some packets of mustard and cress seeds which he planted with our grandson. It helped to reduce his boredom and did not need long spells of concentration. It was a bonus seeing him still able to chat to Thomas – and we ate the produce!'

Paula, carer

'My mother is a great fan of the TV soap programmes but she often lost track of time and forgot to watch. I started to give her a quick telephone call each day to coincide with her favourite programme. It kept me in touch with a daily report of her doings and I stayed on the line until she had switched on the TV.'

When concentration is at a low ebb, don't expect too much from your relative. It is well recognised that people who have lost their powers of attention find intensive activities such as chess and heavy reading virtually impossible. There are many ways to lift the spirit and relieve boredom without being too demanding. A walk in the garden or along the pavement for a few minutes, chatting and remembering about different plants, may be sufficient. Spend time together talking about childhood times or looking at photograph albums; buy your relative a favourite magazine to browse through, or set up a tape recorder or compact disc player to enable them to listen to music or 'talking books'. Be aware that interaction with other people may be less welcome, so do not arrange social events that will cause distress without asking your relative about the type of activities and company they think they would – or would not – enjoy.

Dr Stuart, consultant geriatrician

'Remember that you are dealing with an adult – perhaps with adult tastes – so don't be too patronising in your approach or offer treats like you might to a child.'

The public library is the best source of information about what's happening locally: most branches carry a wide range of details about services and events, with some specialist facilities targeted at carers. As well as books of all sorts, look out for:

- lists of clubs and hobby groups;
- audio and video tapes;
- mobile and doorstep library services for home delivery of books and tapes to people who experience significant difficulty getting to a library because of illness, disability or caring responsibilities;
- 'Talking News' style services providing a range of interesting items via postal tapes – usually for visually impaired people but often extended to people with other disabilities;
- 'befriending' schemes where volunteers come to the house to chat or play games with people who are temporarily or permanently housebound;
- branches of University of the Third Age (U3A) that offer a vast range of daytime study and recreational classes for people who are older and wish to keep their minds stimulated (see page 175).

Try not to be the only person who acts as companion and chauffeur. Wherever possible, enlist the help of family and friends for all manner of support – from shoppers and drivers to companions and listeners. It would be a sensible move to gauge how your relative feels, however, as you may need to act in a 'gatekeeping' role if offers of help become too overwhelming.

Alternative and complementary treatments

The conventionally-based strategies and support methods described above offer you and your relative some ways in which you can help yourselves. Some people, as part of this self-help philosophy, also seek out other, less well-documented therapies, especially when they feel that established treatments have little to offer. It must be stressed, however, that the examples of non-conventional treatments described below are not 'miracle cures'. Occasionally accounts of spectacular results are reported in the press or promotional books written by practitioners about the benefits of non-orthodox treatments. Unfortunately, despite any public claims there are no proven cures for memory loss. In most cases where far-reaching claims have been made about alternative products, scientifically controlled trials have failed to achieve the same results in other patients.

Generally, complementary treatments are used together with conventional therapy. There is no reason why you and your relative should not find out about, or use, such therapies if you so wish. Sometimes this kind of remedy can bring relief during stressful times for you the carer and your relative; many traditional-type therapies have been practised for centuries bringing emotional and physical relief. Reputable therapists never make direct claims that their methods will cure a disease or a degenerative condition; instead they will support the view that natural therapies may help to promote wellbeing. The important advice is to use the therapies sensibly and to work with the orthodox medical team.

The terms alternative therapy and complementary therapy are used to describe a range of treatments available from practitioners and therapists who work to treat the whole body, in conjunction with conventional medicine or not. In order to clarify the difference in meaning, the following descriptions are commonly accepted.

- **Conventional medicine** This term covers a range of treatments which your relative may have already received, including antibiotic treatment, treatment for hormone deficiency and surgery. These therapies have been widely used throughout the world for many years and have undergone expert clinical trials.

- **Unconventional medicine** This term covers a number of treatments that are widely used and, on the whole, widely respected. Included in this group are homeopathy and herbal medicine.
- **Complementary therapies** These therapies are intended to be used *alongside* (as a complement to), rather than replace orthodox medicine; examples include physical treatments such as massage, as well as treatments that benefit the mental state of mind, such as counselling and psychotherapy.
- **Alternative therapies** This term is generally used for treatments that are given *instead* of conventional treatments. These therapies often involve regimens that attempt to treat the illnesses directly, using non-medical methods; examples include specific diets and megavitamin therapy. Most alternative treatments have not been subjected to clinical trials.

You and your relative may be sceptical about whether these treatments work or not, especially if they rely on less orthodox and 'unseen' methods. Many popular complementary treatments originated in the East and have been practised there for centuries. They rely on ancient knowledge linked to herbal remedies and traditional practices that are believed to stimulate the body's own healing powers; acupuncture from China and yoga from India are obvious examples. Some of the newer therapies appeal more to Western scientific minds and are used as aids to diagnosis as well as treatment. Two examples are colour therapy, that draws links between certain colours and mental harmony or stress, and iridology that examines the eyes for clues to hidden disorders.

Kathy, carer

'While my husband was at his day centre, after his stroke, I went to our local health centre to have very simple aromatherapy for myself. The practice nurse suggested it and it was wonderful. I was a bit unsure about going alone so my sister came along with me. I told myself it was my treat to me.'

All complementary and alternative treatments can be obtained without going to a medically trained doctor but this does not mean that an NHS or private doctor will not or cannot provide some complementary treatments; some doctors are dually trained and GPs are beginning to recommend the benefits of such therapies. Increasingly, complementary therapies are being introduced into the NHS and are available at day centres and GP practices, either free of charge or with a fee. Geographical location may affect your ability to find a suitable practitioner. Ask at your local library or GP practice or contact the national organisations listed in the sections 'For more information'.

Daniel, general practitioner

'Don't keep it a secret if you are finding benefits from other therapies – most of us doctors are broad minded and we like to know what else works.'

A note of caution Before using any complementary or alternative therapy with your relative, especially if they are undertaking other treatments, such as chemotherapy, it is extremely important to consult with their GP. There are several reasons for seeking advice before starting a non-orthodox treatment: some therapies use extracts from plants that can have very powerful properties that may affect other treatments; the effort of being massaged may be too tiring for a weakened body; and some therapies use methods that have not been scientifically tested. There is some conflict of opinion between supporters of conventional medicine and supporters of alternative therapies; many doctors providing orthodox treatment are concerned that alternative cures may be harmful or their use (without proper consultation) could delay diagnosis of an illness.

Finding a qualified therapist

Several of the therapies described below can be practised at home using basic remedies and techniques learned from a book. There are some ready made treatments available in health shops. However, rather than spend time learning new techniques you and your relative may prefer to receive treatment from a qualified practitioner. Some alternative therapies cannot be recommended for self-help practice and it is advisable that treatment is obtained only from a trained practitioner. Word of mouth can be a good form of recommendation but do make sure any therapist you visit is registered to practice with the appropriate national body.

Don't be embarrassed to ask directly about qualifications, as all trained therapists will be pleased to offer reassurance and tell you how to check. Properly trained therapists take a full medical history before prescribing and have learned about the dosage and combinations of herbs, whereas untrained people can only guess and may do harm. If you use information from a book to prepare treatment materials, be sure to follow the instructions carefully. Finally, whichever alternative treatment you choose it is wise to consult a medical doctor if symptoms persist.

The non-traditional treatments listed below are given as examples only and do not cover the full range of therapies. They are all viewed as 'complementary' therapies, no 'alternative' therapies have been included.

- **Acupressure** This is an ancient skill practised in China and Japan for over 3,000 years. It combines massage with acupuncture principles and is thought to have been the forerunner of acupuncture. It does not use needles. Acupressure is believed to improve the body's healing powers, prevent illness and promote energy. Practitioners work on known pressure points with thumbs, fingertips, etc, to balance the flow of energy called *Qi*, which runs throughout the body via meridians or invisible channels. Acupressure relieves the symptoms of many conditions and is best used in conjunction with other natural or orthodox treatments.
- **Aromatherapy** This therapy combines the restorative properties of aromatic plant essences with the soothing effects of gentle massage. It is a good therapy to try if complementary treatments are new to you, and products and practitioners tend to be widely available. Aromatherapy is an ancient art and its gentle methods encourage a

relaxed feeling. A trained therapist will ask questions first to discover the best treatment for each individual person. The essential oils can be used either singly or in combination, and are absorbed through the skin where they pass through the tissues to the bloodstream and so travel around the body. They are used in concentrations that are many times stronger than their original plant form and are rarely used undiluted because they are too powerful to use directly on the skin. It is important to be aware of the potency of essential oils and that their use is not advised with people who suffer from certain conditions, in particular, a history of miscarriage, haemophilia, advanced varicose veins or a high temperature. Always read the instructions carefully before use or follow the advice of a therapist. Aromatherapy oils should *never* be taken by mouth

- **Bach Flower Remedies** These remedies are named after the medical and homeopathic trained doctor who researched the healing power of plants in the 1930s. He believed that the characteristics of disorders, whether physical or psychological, could be treated by a cure drawn from plants, sunlight, spring water and fresh air. People have always made use of medicinal herbs, but the thirty-eight Bach Remedies claim to use the essential energy within the plant rather than actual plant material. In practice the Remedies tend to be used to treat psychological symptoms. This does not imply that the conditions are imagined, simply that they stem from whole body experiences that affect the mind as well as the body.

- **Faith healing** This form of healing is based on the belief that positive or 'right' thinking can cure or relieve illness. The belief is particularly strong when practised within a religious setting where healing through spiritual means is preached. Patients are attended by non-medical healers, who believe that faith healing enhances the body's natural defences by reducing the effects of stress. It can reinforce the mental attitude of patients so that they feel better, even though their condition may not be improved.

- **Homeopathy** This therapy relies on the principle of 'treating like with like' whereby minute quantities of natural substances are given to stimulate the body's own healing power. The practice is centuries old and is widely used as the sole form of treatment or as a complement to orthodox medicine. The name 'homeopathy' is derived from two Greek words – 'homoeos' (similar) and 'pathos' (disease). Patients are given minute doses of substances that, in a healthy person, would cause similar signs and symptoms to those presented by the ill person. By creating a similar condition the homeopathic remedy stimulates the body to heal itself. The skill lies in knowing the potency of the substances and matching these to the specific signs and symptom described by the patient. Treatments are prescribed individually.

- **Reflexology** This is a physical therapy that involves massaging areas of the body (mainly the feet) which practitioners believe helps to free blockages in energy pathways. It is a relaxing therapy which relies on the healing power of touch rather than substances; at the end of each session people usually feel very warm and contented. The method has been used for several thousand years and is described in ancient Chinese and Egyptian writings. The reflex points on the feet (or hands) are laid out to form a 'map' of the body, the right and left feet reflecting the right and left sides. A reflexologist takes a full history from the person and uses both feet to give whole body treatment. It's an ideal way to boost circulation. Areas in the foot, which feel especially tender when massaged, could indicate a degree of imbalance in the body. The skill of the reflexologist lies in their ability to interpret the tenderness and apply the correct pressure, bearing in mind that some people have more sensitive feet than others.

Other therapies

There are many other types of therapies which can be used to complement each other and orthodox medicine. You can find out more about them at your local library:

- **Chiropractic and osteopathy** Both of these therapies relieve pain through joint manipulation and are used widely in orthodox medicine.
- **Herbal medicine** This is a treatment approach that uses the potent healing properties of plants.

Note These preparations must always be used with caution! Like all drugs, they can have unwanted (side) effects.

- **Hypnotherapy** Hypnotherapy induces a trance-like state to bring about physical and mental changes.
- **Hydrotherapy** This involves the use of water treatments, to purify and heal the body.
- **Shiatsu** This Japanese form of massage is based on the idea that good health depends on a balanced flow of energy through specific channels in the body.
- **T'ai-chi Ch'uan** This is a form of meditation in motion.

For more information

The following organisations would all give you advice and supply you with further details of specialist organisations (see the 'Useful addresses' section at the end of the book) or ask at your local library:

- British Holistic Medical Association (BHMA).

- Centre for Study of Complementary Medicine.

- Council for Complementary and Alternative Medicine.

- Institute of Complementary Medicine.

- National College of Hypnosis and Psychotherapy.

- National Federation of Spiritual Healers.

- Society for the Promotion of Nutritional Therapy.

- *Readers Digest Family Guide to Alternative Medicine*, published by Reader's Digest.

- *Know Your Complementary Therapies*, by Eileen Inge Herzberg, published by Age Concern Books.

Conclusion

This chapter has focused on general health because keeping healthy matters enormously, whatever the state of your relative's memory. Being fit cannot alter basic memory dysfunction, and is unlikely to affect its progress, but it might help to sort out some of the other exacerbating factors. For example, a poor diet with an erratic eating pattern could mean that blood sugar levels fluctuate and this can make a person feel very irritable. Fewer problems means lower stress levels for everybody. The next chapter takes a look at the financial and legal affairs of an older person.

For more information

- *i* Age Concern Factsheet 45 *Staying healthy in later life*.

- *i* Ask at your doctor's surgery or health centre, as most practices keep a very comprehensive range of general health information.

- *i* Local public libraries and most good bookshops keep general, health-related books.

6 Dealing with personal affairs

Helping to manage the financial and legal affairs of another person is one of the main roles of a carer. This can be for a number of reasons: because their relative has become too mentally unwell or physically disabled to manage alone; because they feel unsure about dealing with people in 'authority'; or because they no longer wish to take decisions alone about complex issues. The time span involved in taking over responsibility may be gradual or swift, depending on the state of health and wishes of your relative.

This chapter outlines the services and agencies you could turn to for help, and describes some of the welfare benefits and legal procedures that you and your relative may wish to investigate. It is unlikely that you will require all of the information at any one time so return to the relevant sections as necessary during your relative's illness. One section, however, that you may wish to find out more about immediately, is that relating to 'living wills' – a form of advance directive which enables people to set out their wishes about the manner in which they die – within legal boundaries.

Dealing with the affairs of another person is a serious business and you may feel unsure at first where to start. However, there are people who will help you and there are many safeguards in place to protect both you and your relative. Always cover yourself by seeking advice from a reputable source – a solicitor, an accountant, a bank or a voluntary organisation – before you enter into legal contracts or make major decisions, especially concerning property or the management of your relative's money, or Power of Attorney/Enduring Power of Attorney.

Jeanne, carer

'After my husband's memory began to fail I took over our financial affairs. The accountant did our tax self-assessment forms and I talked to the financial adviser about his health insurance policy.'

Finding out about help and advice

Getting the right information needs mental stamina, creative thinking and the investigative skills of Sherlock Holmes – or so it can feel on occasions, particularly if you are tied to the house. With perseverance, however, you can be well informed. Look out for informative articles published by the local and national press, check the listed programmes to be broadcast on radio and television and investigate the huge range of information available on the various websites. If you do not have access to the Internet yourself, this is an area where a younger family member or friend would no doubt be keen to demonstrate their knowledge and skills! Alternatively, the majority of public libraries provide Internet points and someone would help you go 'on-line'. This type of media material is mostly well researched and aimed at the general public. For more detailed information, advice and advocacy there are many local and national organisations that offer carers a service. Some are specialists in their field while others provide general information and act as signposts to the specialists. Most organisations offer facilities for older and disabled people and some information is available in minority languages. If time is precious ask a friend to investigate on your behalf. The main agencies to contact are listed in the table below.

Charles, carer

'Brenda had always done the day to day household finances, so when she began to mislay the bills I had to think about budgeting the money. To save myself a journey to the post office I changed our pensions to go straight into our bank account and set up monthly payments for all the main bills.'

Emily, carer

'When my husband stopped being the one who managed the money I got in a bit of a muddle paying the bills. So my neighbour went with me to the Citizens Advice Bureau and they quickly helped me sort it out.'

Organisation	Services offered	How to contact
Advocacy services	Independent organisations that support citizens advocacy work with people who need help controlling their affairs	Local telephone directory or ask at CAB
Age Concern	Can provide information, support, practical help, social activities and a range of publications for older people and carers	Local telephone directory or address on page 177
Benefits Agency/ Pensions Services (now known as the Department for Work and Pensions)	Provides information on all welfare benefits and processes most local claims	Local telephone directory
Benefits Enquiry Freephone Line	Provides general advice, information, claim forms and leaflets for disabled people and their carers by telephone or post but cannot deal with individual claims	Tel: 0800 882200 Textphone: 0800 243355

89

Benefits Advice Centres (Independent)	Independent organisations in many urban areas and some rural areas offering free advice on problems relating to benefits, debt and work issues	Local telephone directory
Citizens Advice Bureaux	Free, confidential advice and information on a wide range of legal, financial, social and consumer problems and help with form filling and representation at hearings	Local telephone directory
Counsel and Care	Provides free counselling, information and advice for older people and carers, publishes a range of factsheets and administers trust funds that make payments for equipment and respite care	Address on page 166
Disability Information Services (called DIAL in some areas)	Advice on aids, equipment and services	Local telephone directory
Disabled Living Centres Council	Information on Disabled Living Centres near you	Address on page 167
Disabled Living Foundation	Advice on aids and equipment	Address on page 168
Help the Aged	Provides a range of services including Seniorline (a free information helpline)	Address on page 169
Housing Advice	Many local councils provide a housing advice service to local residents in private or rented accommodation	Local telephone directory

Neighbourhood Schemes	Many local councils run community schemes offering a range of information and support to local people	Local telephone directory under Council
NHS Direct	Provides confidential health advice and information, 24 hours a day, seven days a week. Helplines are staffed by qualified nurses and health advisers	Telephone 0845 4647
PALS (Patient Advice and Liaison Service)	Your local Primary Care Trust (the body responsible for family health services) should have a PALS Manager who you can contact (by telephone initially) for advice	Ask at your doctor's surgery or health centre
Public Library	Excellent sources of local information, books, videos, directories, quality journals and many daily newspapers	Personal visit, telephone, or limited home delivery
The Pension Service	Delivers services and products through a network of pension centres across England, Scotland and Wales.	Telephone 0845 606 0285 to be connected with the pension centre covering your area

State benefits and grants

The benefits system is complex and can only be covered broadly here because each person has individual needs and the information, amounts given and eligibility is subject to change. The Department for Work and Pensions (DWP, formerly the Department of Social Security) is the government agency responsible for social security and benefits.

The benefits listed on the following pages are those most applicable to an older age group. The full range of benefits available to all age groups can be found in a selection of leaflets available from the DWP, most local authorities, the Citizens Advice Bureaux and some post offices. Useful ones to look out for are:

- DWP leaflet SD4 *Caring for Someone*, including carers' benefits.
- DWP leaflet SD1 *Sick or Disabled?*

For telephone advice about claims and information contact the **Benefits Enquiry Line** (see page 89). If you need information about benefits in other languages contact your local DWP office (see telephone directory).

People claiming a benefit must meet strict criteria. Some benefits are means-tested or taxed or both. Changes in the benefits system also mean that certain tax credits might be available to people aged 60 years and above, as well as eligible families. If you or your relative disagrees with a decision made by the DWP, you have the right to appeal and ask for your case to be looked at again. There are strict deadlines for lodging an appeal so, if you are concerned, you should seek advice urgently.

John, a Benefits Adviser

'Ask about benefits or you won't know what is currently available. It's really worth getting a knowledgeable person to check out your circumstances. Ask for help at the Citizens Advice Bureau.'

Why are people reluctant to claim?

There are millions of pounds of unclaimed benefits, particularly those targeted at older people. Benefits Advisers say that older people and carers are reluctant to claim means-tested benefits, and many carers claim on behalf of a relative without realising that they might be eligible for benefits in their own right. The list below gives some reasons why eligible people do not make a claim:

- they think they are not entitled to money;
- they don't know what is available;
- they are too proud and believe that they may be taking money from someone else who is more deserving;
- they don't want to be bothered with the paperwork;
- they find the claim forms too complicated.

Margaret, a Benefits Adviser

'Many older people and carers say that they feel too tired and busy to think about benefits. They continue to struggle and try to manage when they may be entitled to make a claim; it's OK to ask for help.'

Benefits for older or disabled people

Attendance Allowance

Attendance Allowance is for people aged 65 years or over (whether or not they live alone) who need help with personal care supervision or someone to watch over them. It is tax free and not means-tested and not dependent on National Insurance contributions. But in order to qualify, the person must normally have needed help with personal care for a period of six months.

If Attendance Allowance is granted, it will be backdated to the date of the claim as long as the six months qualifying period has been satisfied. However, people who are terminally ill qualify immediately. There are two rates according to how much care is needed. Get a claim pack (AA1) containing leaflet DS 702 from the DWP office, or by telephoning the Benefits Enquiry Line (see the Table on page 89). You could also contact one of the advice agencies (such as the Citizens Advice Bureau), which may able to help your relative fill it in.

Disability Living Allowance (DLA)

Disability Living Allowance is for people who claim before they reach the age of 65, and who have needed care or had mobility difficulties for more than three months. It has a care component for people who need help with personal care supervision or someone to watch over them, and a mobility component for people who need help with getting around. Disability Living Allowance is tax free and not means-tested, nor is it dependent on National Insurance contributions. The person receiving the allowance is free to spend the money however they choose; it does not have to be spent on care. The mobility component has two rates and the care component three; these are awarded according to the needs of the disabled person. People who are terminally ill qualify immediately for the highest rate of the care component. The Disability Living Allowance is a gateway to other types of help (eg the Blue Badge scheme, which gives holders special parking privileges – see Leaflet DS 704).

Incapacity Benefit (IB)

Incapacity Benefit is for people under state pension age who are unable to work because of an illness or disability, and have paid enough National Insurance contributions. The benefit is given at different rates, depending on how long the person has been unable to work. For the first 28 weeks a claimant is assessed on their ability to carry out their own job, based on information given on medical certificates provided by the GP. After 28 weeks the sick or disabled person is assessed on how well they can carry out a range of work related activities, called the Personal Capability Assessment. This assessment is carried out after the claimant completes a questionnaire and possibly also an examination by an appointed doctor. Some people may qualify for extra money if their husband or wife is over 60 years old, or if they have dependent children (see Leaflet IB 1).

Benefits for carers

Carers' Allowance (CA)

To qualify for Carers' Allowance you must be providing care for at least 35 hours per week to a person who is receiving Attendance Allowance *or* Constant Attendance Allowance *or* the middle or highest rates of the care component of Disability Living Allowance. You must be aged 16 or over and under 65 years when you first claim. You cannot get Carers' Allowance if you are in full-time education. You can have a job and still get Carers' Allowance but must not earn above a certain amount (after deduction of allowable expenses). The allowance is taxable. You may be able to get help with the cost of another carer if you work and you may be able to get extra money added to other benefits which you are eligible to receive. Carers' Allowance can be backdated for three months (see Leaflet DS 700).

The Carer Premium/Addition

This is an extra amount of money paid to a carer as part of their Income Support, Pension Credit, Housing Benefit or Council Tax Benefit. You will be entitled to the Carer Premium if you are entitled to Carers' Allowance (even if you don't get Carers' Allowance because you are already getting a state pension or other benefits).

Home Responsibilities Protection (HRP)

Home Responsibilities Protection is not a true benefit but a scheme which helps protect your basic retirement pension. If you are unable to pay National Insurance contributions or have not paid enough for any year of caring, you can apply for HRP, which helps towards qualifying for retirement pension. If you receive Carers' Allowance, you are entitled to National Insurance credits (free contributions on your NI record) and will not usually need HRP. If you get Income Support because you are caring for someone, you will usually get HRP automatically. If you cannot claim Carers' Allowance for any reason but still care for over 35 hours per week for someone who receives Attendance Allowance, Constant Attendance Allowance or high or middle rate of the care component of Disability Living Allowance, you may be able to get HRP. Ask at the local Jobcentre Plus office for Form CF411.

General benefits

Income Support (Minimum Income Guarantee)

Income Support is a means-tested benefit paid to people aged between 16 and 60 years, whose income is below a certain level and who are not expected to sign on as unemployed. It is paid to people who do not have to sign on for work, for example people who can't work because they are carers, or people who are sick or disabled. Income Support can be paid to top up other benefits or earnings from part-time work (including self-employment), provided they work fewer than 16 hours per week. To claim, contact your local Jobcentre Plus office.

Housing Benefit and Council Tax Benefit

These benefits are worked out in a similar way to Income Support but are administered by the local Council (see below). Savings and some income may affect how much you or your relative can get. Housing Benefit helps tenants pay rent and Council Tax Benefit helps tenants and home owners pay their Council Tax. People receiving Income Support and who claim Housing Benefit or Council Tax Benefit will generally automatically be awarded the maximum amounts (see Leaflet RR2).

Pension Credit

Pension Credit is a social security entitlement for people aged 60 and over, introduced in October 2003. It guarantees that everyone within this age group is entitled to receive a weekly income above a desig-nated level. You do not need to have paid National Insurance contributions to qualify for Pension Credit, but your income and any savings and capital over a certain level will be taken into account. It is not taxable.

It has two parts – the guarantee credit and the savings credit. The guarantee credit has replaced Income Support for people aged 60 and over. It tops up income to a designated level. Unlike Income Support, there is no upper savings level. The savings credit is intended to reward people aged 64 and over for a proportion of the savings and income they have for their retirement. (In the past, older people who had saved towards their retirement were no better off than those who had not saved.) People may be entitled to the guarantee credit, or the savings credit, or both.

For a couple, one of you applies on behalf of both partners (a partner means a spouse or two people who live together as if married to each other). The person who applies for Pension Credit must be at least 60 years of age; it does not matter if their partner is under 60. To qualify for the savings credit, at least one of you must be 65 or over.

To qualify for Pension Credit, the person is subject to an assessment of weekly net income (after deductions) and savings. Only certain types of income are counted, including pensions, state benefits (eg Carer's Allowance) and earnings from a job. Some benefits are not taken into account, including Attendance Allowance and Disability Living Allowance. The amount of savings a person has is taken into account. There are higher rates of Pension Credit for certain groups of people (those who are severely disabled, carers of severely disabled people and those who have certain housing costs). There is a special Pension Credit line on 0800 99 1234, but if you prefer you can contact a local advice agency or the local Pension Service.

Pension Credit replaced Minimum Income Guarantee (MIG).

The Social Fund

The Social Fund provides grants and loans to help people with expenses that are difficult to pay for out of regular income. (Leaflet

GL18 covers benefits listed below.) Budgeting Loans, Crisis Loans and Community Care Grants are discretionary, but the other payments described below are made to everyone who satisfies the conditions.

Budgeting Loans

Budgeting Loans may be available to people receiving Income Support or certain other benefits (for at least 26 weeks) to help spread the cost of important expenses. Interest-free loans (which have to be paid back) may be available for items such as furniture, clothing or to pay travel expenses.

Crisis Loans

Crisis Loans are for people with no savings or access to funds to help them cope with an emergency or disaster (such as fire or a burglary) that puts the family at serious health or safety risk. Applicants do not have to be in receipt of other benefits. The interest-free loan has to be paid back.

Community Care Grants

These grants are available to people on Pension Credit and certain other State benefits, and to people who will be discharged from care within six weeks and are likely to receive these benefits on discharge. The grants do not have to be repaid, but the amount of any savings over £1,000 (£500 for people under 60) will be deducted from the grant. The grants are available for purposes such as help with moving out of care, or to enable someone to remain living at home.

Cold Weather Payments

Cold Weather Payments are paid automatically to some recipients of Income Support, including pensioners and disabled people, when the actual or forecast temperature goes down to freezing (zero degrees Celsius) or below, for seven consecutive days.

Winter Fuel Payments

Winter Fuel Payment is a one-off annual payment towards the heaviest winter fuel bill. It is normally paid automatically to most people aged 60 years and over, although some need to make an application.

Funeral payment

Help for funeral expenses is available to some people receiving means-tested benefits, who are responsible for the funeral of a partner, close relative or close friend. The payment may have to be repaid from any money or property left by the person who died. The DWP must agree that it is reasonable for the person to be responsible for the funeral before they will agree any payment so it is important to check before making arrangements.

Bereavement benefits

People widowed below pension age may be entitled to bereavement benefits such as the Bereavement Payment or Bereavement Allowance (see Leaflet GL14).

For more information

- *i* Age Concern Information Sheet 16 *Changes to Pension and Benefit Payments.*
- *i* Age Concern Factsheet 17 *Housing Benefit and Council Tax Benefit.*
- *i* Age Concern Factsheet 18 *A brief guide to money benefits.*
- *i* Age Concern Factsheet 25 *Income Support/Minimum Income guarantee and the Social Fund.*
- *i* Age Concern Factsheet 34 *Attendance Allowance and Disability Living Allowance.*
- *i* Age Concern Factsheet 48 *Pension Credit.*
- *i* Age Concern Factsheet 49 *Help from the Social Fund.*
- *i* Age Concern Books *Your Rights: a guide to benefits for older people* (see page 178).

ⓘ The Pensions Service has its own information line: 0800 99 1234 (Textphone: 0800 169 0133). The line is open from 8am to 8pm Monday to Friday, and 9am to 1pm on Saturday.

NHS benefits

A range of health-related benefits is available for people who receive other state benefits or are on a low income. These might help your relative with charges for prescriptions, eye tests and glasses, dentures and dental treatment, wigs and fabric supports (such as bandage-type supports and elastic stockings) as well as with fares to hospital for receiving NHS treatment. Some people (such as those on Income Support) are automatically exempted from some of these charges. Other people on a low income may get help if they apply on form HC1 (except for hospital fares to hospital, which must be claimed from the hospital at each visit). Ask for details at your surgery, hospital clinic or a pharmacy.

For more information

ⓘ *Advisor's Guide to help with health costs* (NHS booklet HC13) available on the NHS website at www.doh.gov.uk.

ⓘ Health Benefits Division of NHS, Tel: 0845 6018076.

Taxation

Inland Revenue

Home visits can be arranged for enquiries about personal income and other taxes if your relative is unable to get to a local office. A range of information is available in booklets, many of which appear in other languages, Braille and large print, and in audio cassettes.

Council Tax

Council Tax, collected by local authorities as a contribution towards local services, is assessed according to the value of each property and the number of adults in it. There are reductions, discounts and exemptions available that may help you as a carer and your relative. These relate to empty dwellings (you may have left your home to go and care for your relative or they may have moved in with you), to homes with substantial adaptations that are placed in a lower valuation band, and to people whose presence in a household is disregarded, so leading to a lower bill. Once your Council Tax liability is assessed you or your relative may be able to claim Council Tax Benefit (see above) to help pay. Get help from an advice agency (see the table on pages 89–91) or your local authority.

For more information

ℹ Age Concern Factsheet 15 *Income Tax and older people*.

ℹ Age Concern Factsheet 21 *Council Tax and older people*.

ℹ Age Concern Books *Your Rights: A guide to money benefits for older people*, published annually (see page 180).

Grants from private organisations

Many charitable trusts and foundations offer grants to help purchase one-off items of equipment, or pay for respite care. The qualifying criteria vary; for example, a trust fund may be open only to certain categories of people living in a defined area. For information about local and national grant-making organisations try asking at the Citizens Advice Bureau or public library, or contact Counsel and Care (see page 166) or the National Association of Councils for Voluntary Service (see page 171). Occasionally parish councils administer trusts set up by a local benefactor.

Managing another person's financial affairs

There are several ways that you can take over responsibility for your relative's financial affairs, depending on their physical and mental health status. Their needs may alter rapidly, especially if their memory loss becomes worse, so be ready to increase your level of responsibility and be sure you have set up appropriate procedures before it becomes too late to make changes.

Agents

If your relative is mentally capable (despite a minor degree of memory loss), but unable to get out, they can retain overall responsibility for their money but appoint you as their agent. You would be able to cash any pensions and benefits and you may be able to arrange a third party mandate to enable you to deal with bank and building society accounts on their behalf. Ask for details at a post office or bank, as many organisations have a standard application form.

Powers of Attorney

If your relative has financial affairs, you may have to consider a *Power of Attorney*, which is a legal procedure to enable you to deal with their money. The *Ordinary* Power of Attorney can be set up for cases where the person is able to give sound instructions; however, it will become invalid if the person becomes mentally incapable. To avoid this problem, most solicitors suggest an *Enduring* Power of Attorney, which can continue to be used even if your relative becomes too confused to manage their own affairs provided it is registered with the Public Guardianship office. It is important that you each take independent advice before setting this up, as it carries a heavy responsibility for the carer that could involve selling property and dealing with taxation. The procedure is very formal so, although not essential, it is usual to act through a solicitor. Further information can be obtained from the Public Guardianship Office (address on page 172).

Court of Protection

If your relative is already 'mentally incapable' the action you can take will depend on their income. For state benefits only, you can become their *appointee*, a procedure that allows you to manage everything to do with their benefits. If the situation is more complex and you do not already have enduring power of attorney you can apply to the Court of Protection. It will appoint a receiver (usually a relative) to manage all the financial business. If you do not wish to undertake this duty, a bank or solicitor will act as receiver in your place. Contact the Customer Services Unit of the Public Guardianship Office (see page 173).

For more information

ⓘ Age Concern Factsheet 22 *Legal arrangements for managing financial affairs.*

Managing financial affairs in Scotland

The Adults with Incapacity (Scotland) Act 2000 changed the law relating to the management of financial affairs from April 2001. Individuals can arrange for their welfare to be safeguarded and their affairs to be properly managed in the future, should their capacity deteriorate. They do this by giving another person the Power of Attorney to look after their affairs.

All continuing and welfare Powers of Attorney granted after April 2001 will need to be registered with the Public Guardian Office to be effective. Individuals can also apply to the Public Guardian Office to access the funds of an adult incapable of managing these funds. From April 2002, authorised care establishments can manage a limited amount of funds and property of residents who are unable to do this for themselves.

For more information

ⓘ See the Scottish version of Age Concern Factsheet 22 *Legal arrangements for managing financial affairs.*

Making a will

John, a solicitor

'Death is always a difficult subject to deal with but making a will and other financial arrangements can save a lot of heartache in the long run.'

When someone is ill, they begin to think more about their personal affairs and may ask you to help them sort out the legal arrangements. Your relative may talk to you about making a will, or they may wish to add to or alter an existing will, if their situation has changed. If you feel uncomfortable or unsure about doing this task, ask someone else to help – perhaps a friend who is sensible and practical but less personally involved. If your relative is unable to go out, many solicitors offer a home service to help people write a will. Look in the *Yellow Pages* or ask at the Citizens Advice Bureau for details.

Some people draw up their own wills. This is quite in order as long as the correct procedures are followed. The will must be written clearly, and signed and dated in the presence of two (or just one in Scotland) independent witnesses or relatives who are not beneficiaries, and must not be married to a beneficiary. The will should name at least one person who is willing to act as an executor – the people responsible for seeing that the instructions written in the will are properly carried out. Executors can be relatives, friends or professional people, who provide this service as part of their job (eg an accountant or solicitor). A person who acts as an executor can also be named in the will as a beneficiary. Information packs and will forms are available from most stationers, and details of other booklets are given below. (If you live in Scotland make sure that the information covers the law in Scotland.) If your relative's affairs are not simple or straightforward, it would be wise to ask a solicitor to draw up the will. Solicitors' fees for home and office appointments vary, so telephone and ask for a price guide before booking a home visit.

Why is making a will important?

Some people wrongly assume that if their affairs are straightforward they do not need to make a will, because all of their belongings will go directly to their closest relative. But there are strict laws about how a person's estate (the name given to their possessions) is divided up and it can be complicated and costly to sort out the affairs of someone who has died without making a will ('intestate').

The following sensible comments from a solicitor should help if your relative is undecided and asks your opinion about the benefits of making a will.

Paul, a legal adviser

- 'You don't have to have a lot of money to make a will. Making a will is about making sure that your possessions go to the person(s) you want to receive them.'

- 'You mustn't feel morbid about making a will; all you are doing is setting out your plan as to how your assets are to be split up when you die.'

- 'If you do not make a will the rules governing intestacy apply, which may mean that your assets will be given to relatives you do not know or even want to know.'

- 'Just saying to someone that a treasured ornament or a piece of jewellery is theirs when you die is not good enough. The only safe way of making sure that happens is to put it in a will.'

A 'living will' – an advance directive

Daniel, a general practitioner

'I always take account of a good, advance directive when caring for a patient who is in a potentially terminal phase. Doctors believe they are a help rather than a hindrance.'

Do not be afraid to talk with your relative openly about their wishes in matters surrounding their death as it is very probable that they will wish to share their feelings with someone close to them. Many people feel the need to attend to their affairs sensibly whilst they are capable of thinking coherently. A phrase often used to describe this period is 'putting your house in order'. An 'advance directive' – a form of living will is an example of this type of forward planning which covers, specifically, a person's desire to exercise some control over the manner in which they die – within legal boundaries. However, with the taboos that still persist about death, many people do not always find it easy to broach the topic. Inevitably, some people never have the opportunity to make their wishes known, leading to the situation where they die in circumstances that are less than ideal for them.

Policy statement, Age Concern England, September 2002

'Older people should have access to quality palliative care services (including pain management) which support their physical and mental wellbeing, respect their personal choice (including where directives are made) and maintain their dignity.'

In recent years living wills have been actively promoted by organisations and professional people, as a means of giving individuals some pre-considered choice about such issues as medical treatment. At the time of writing there is no primary legislation covering advance directives, and there is no guarantee that people who have made such a statement will achieve their wishes. However, case law does support adherence to these and common law does confirm the principle of consent for treatment and therefore the importance of taking into account any statements made by the patient.

The National Funerals College has drawn up a charter stating what it believes are the rights of people who are preparing for death. The charter covers their right to:

- exercise informed choice;
- be confident that expressed wishes will be respected;
- expect that survivors will be helped and supported in the future;
- expect post-funeral care of graves and memorials.

(In addition the charter calls for a form of legal registration for funeral directors.)

It is not necessary to use a lawyer to prepare an advance directive. However, the ethical, legal and practical issues are complex, so no person or family should attempt to draw up a document without first researching the topic thoroughly and taking some form of professional advice. For example, the Age Concern England information sheet or book on the topic (see below) and the Citizens Advice Bureau would be good starting points. Box 7 below gives a brief example of one of the subject areas a family would need to understand. It would be very important to discuss the situation with your relative's doctor at an early stage of the process. Their GP knows their health history well and can help families understand the treatment choices that might need to be faced. It is also vital that all health professionals know about the statement and can understand the wishes it contains.

Box 7 A valid advance directive requires:

1   Evidence that the person was competent at the time of writing it

2   Evidence that the person is fully informed about the nature of their directive and its implications

3   Evidence that the person has made the decision outlined in the advance directive without pressure or coercion

4   Evidence that the directive has not been changed.

Taken from *Their Rights: Advance directives and living wills explored*, Age Concern England

---

For more information

i Age Concern Information Sheet 5 *Advance statements, advance directives and living wills.*

i Age Concern Books *Their Rights: Advance directives and living wills explored*, by Kevin Kendrick and Simon Robinson (see page 180).

i The British Medical Association (BMA) has produced a report on the topic (published April 1995) called *Advanced Statements about Medical Treatment: Code of Practice with Explanatory Notes* (see page 164 for address). The 'statement' is reproduced in full as Appendix 1 (by permission of the BMA) in the Age Concern book mentioned above.

i The Nursing Times book *Living Wills*, by Linda Wilson (published 1999).

Registering a death

A death should be registered in the district where the death occurred, within five days, unless the Registrar says this period can be extended. The person registering the death can make a formal declaration giving the details required in any registration district in England and Wales. This will then be passed to the registrar for the district where the death occurred, who will issue the death certificate and any other documentation. (In Scotland, the death can be registered in the office for the area where the deceased person normally lived). Some offices operate an appointment system, so telephone as soon as you receive the Medical Certificate of Cause of Death. Whether the death occurs in a hospice or at home you will be given the same type of Certificate. The address and telephone number of the local office are in the telephone directory; leaflets are available from the office.

In certain circumstances, the death will be referred to the Coroner. If this is the case you will be advised what to do. A Coroner is usually involved when the death is sudden, unnatural, unexplained, or attended by suspicious circumstances. However, a common reason is because the GP has not seen the person during the 14 days before their death.

It is usual for the death to be registered by a relative, but this can be done by another person. Allow a reasonable amount of time to complete the formalities, though it will help if you can have certain pieces of information to hand. The Registrar will want to know the following information about the deceased person:

- the date and place of death;
- their full name (and maiden name if appropriate);
- their date and place of birth;
- their occupation and that of the husband for a married women or widow;
- their usual address;
- whether they were in receipt of a pension from public funds;
- the date of birth of their spouse if appropriate;
- their NHS number or actual medical card if available.

Certificates

There are three types of certificates issued by the Registrar depending on who must be told of the death. By law, Registrars cannot issue the necessary certificates unless they are certain beyond all reasonable doubt that the death is above suspicion, particularly if the body is to be cremated.

- **A Certificate for Burial or Cremation (Green Form).** This is supplied for the funeral director who cannot proceed without it. The certificate is free of charge.
- **A Certificate of Registration of Death.** This is supplied for social security purposes. Relatives are asked to read the details on the reverse of the form and return it to the local DWP office if any circumstance applies to the deceased person, for example if they were in receipt of a state pension or welfare benefits. This certificate is free of charge.
- **Standard Death Certificates.** These are issued for use by banks, building societies, insurance companies and any such organisation that requires official notification. It may be wise to buy additional copies at the time of registration as they cost more if a relative re-applies.

For more information

- Age Concern Factsheet 7 *Making your will*.

- Age Concern Factsheet 14 *Dealing with someone's estate*.

- Age Concern Factsheet 22 *Legal arrangements for managing financial affairs*.

- Age Concern Factsheet 27 *Planning a funeral*.

- Age Concern Funeral Plan: a free, information booklet is available. Tel: 0800 38 77 35.

- Benefits Agency booklet D49, *What to do after a death*, available from DWP offices or local probate registry offices.

- The Consumers' Association offer a range of useful information booklets and packs about all aspects of making and dealing with wills (see page 166 for address).

- Contact the local probate registry office (see telephone directory) for information about how to obtain probate. Leaflets are available.

Conclusion

This chapter has covered a wide range of services, available from many organisations and agencies in the private, public and voluntary sectors. If you have read through the chapter briefly, you may find it useful to return to the appropriate section when the time is right, as your relative's circumstances change.

The next chapter offers support and information about how to cope when your relative's memory powers and/or general health begin to worsen.

7 When memory loss worsens and general health deteriorates

However well an older person is cared for, alongside worsening memory powers, their general health may also begin to fail. Although this decline may not be obvious, the wear and tear on internal organs is inevitable and body systems eventually deteriorate. Your personal philosophy for dealing with this situation is a private matter, and you may or may not choose to ask for support. But many of the practical difficulties will be the same for all carers. If the memory loss affecting your relative is getting worse, you are likely to experience additional problems.

This chapter provides useful information to help you make future plans. It may seem difficult or even wrong, to start thinking about failing health before that time arises but many families say it is less stressful to make tentative decisions and plans while they are relatively calm. Talking about the forthcoming period is not morbid, it is a part of the process that helps you all come to terms with changing circumstances.

Caring for an ill person at home is a difficult undertaking which can stir up a mixture of emotions. Carers experience tremendous rewards coupled with extreme tiredness; they feel anxious and sad and frequently become frustrated at the inadequacies of the 'system'. Despite these hurdles, it can often be possible to overcome the problems and many carers feel determined to provide quality care at home for as long as possible.

There are no right or wrong decisions, nor are there effortless ways of dealing with the position. Simply do the best you can, and make use of the help that is available when you feel you have reached that stage.

Short and long term care

New and more experienced carers continually reach stages when they need to break fresh ground – perhaps by taking on increased responsibilities and seeking additional support. The first part of this chapter helps you to assess the type of help you might need. It then guides you through the maze of information about what services are available for older and disabled people and their carers (including for those people whose memory loss has caused more serious mental health deterioration), and how they and you can access the health and social care systems. Later in the chapter, basic material is offered to help you care for your relative as their health worsens.

Do you need help?

Fiona, a carer

'Until I talked to the community nurse I never realised that there were so many organisations that provide support. I would have struggled on alone caring for my father, whereas the help I have received has been tremendous.'

Look at the checklist below and if you answer 'yes' to any of the questions and would like further information, you can ask for help locally. Ask at your surgery, health centre or social services department.

■ Have you just started to care for someone else whose health is failing?

- Do you think the person you care for should have an assessment or re-assessment of their needs?
- Do you want to talk to someone about how you feel and what you are entitled to receive?
- Would you like to know more about respite care facilities?
- Do you feel exhausted and close to breaking point?
- Do you need help to move your relative safely – for either your sake or theirs?
- Do you think extra equipment would help you to manage better?
- Do you feel you have received a poor quality service or support from those providing care?

Rita, community nurse

'If you are unsure about any aspect of caring speak to your community nurse, we can give you lots of information about local services and we can refer you to many agencies – you do not always need to visit the doctor first.'

Even if you have been caring for a while, you may still be unfamiliar with the full range of services. Why not find out what is available before pressure builds up and you reach crisis point? Community nurses or social workers are often thought to be a last point of call, but they can give support and advice to carers long before the crisis stage is reached. The community nurse is one of the key people for accessing other services. In the case of an older person with more severe memory loss it is most likely to be the Mental Health Nurse (sometimes called a Community Psychiatric Nurse or CPN) who works with the person and their family and usually one who specialises in the care of older people.

The assessment process, and how it can help you and your relative, is described in greater detail below. It is the entry point to all types of care and is open to anyone who feels they are in need of a support service. Getting extra help does not mean that you have failed or that you are receiving charity. Families can be surprised and overwhelmed by the speed of change and deterioration in the health of their relative. It is not wrong to make enquiries that show you are anticipating future need.

Being informed

Freda, carers' support worker

'Take a pen and paper with you to make notes when you visit the surgery or any other professional worker. Take your time – although GPs and nurses appear busy people they would not wish you to misunderstand because you are feeling nervous.'

Being informed is a major factor in maintaining control when you are dealing with difficult issues. Knowing what might be offered, even if you are a bit hazy, makes a basic starting point when you seek additional support. Don't try to remember everything you are told but do try to make a note of the key headings that services fall under. For example, your rights as a carer, domestic help, where you can obtain equipment. If your relative is terminally ill, help and support should be available immediately. Gathering information now could save time later, and give you peace of mind when your energies are needed elsewhere. Set up an information folder and keep a notebook if it will help organise your affairs.

Joseph, general practitioner

'The surgery is one of the first places to ask for help. Keep "knocking on the door" if you feel frustrated about getting an answer – you sometimes need to make your GP understand what you want. GPs should be a signpost to other services, and if you find it difficult to get your relative to a surgery tell the receptionist why.'

Local support services

Support for you as a carer and for your relative is available locally from a number of sources run by statutory, private and voluntary organisations. Most of these services can be accessed via the NHS or the social services departments, and your relative will be assessed as requiring 'nursing' care or 'personal' care. There may seem to be little difference in practical terms, and in reality the services try to work very closely together. However, it does make a difference to the way the need for care is assessed and how care is paid for. Changes in care provision brought about after a top-level inquiry has resulted in a National Service Framework which sets out standards of care for older people, whether they are being cared for at home, in a care home or in hospital. There are numerous procedures (and promises) governed by this Framework, which came into effect in April 2001. It includes a one-stop assessment process for health and care in a care home, and new legislation that helps to ease the financial burden of long term care in a care home. It is not possible to outline all of the procedures here so carers are advised to ask for a fuller explanation, from the appropriate authority, when they are making decisions about care requirements. Many agencies use contract workers but all care is regulated by the National Care Standards Commission under the Care Standards Act (England) 2000 and Regulations of Care (Scotland) 2001.

Charges

Charges for care homes vary according to the type of care provided. Since October 2001, registered nursing care is free in any setting in England and Wales. In Scotland, personal care (in addition to nursing care) for those aged 65 or over is also free. If State financial help is not required, private homes are available without undergoing an assessment. However, even if your relative is willing and able to meet the full fees, it is still a good idea to ask for an assessment from social services to help you choose the right sort of home and ensure that all the options are clear. A formal assessment is also important well in advance of a time that financial help is likely to be required if your relative's money is running out. Up-to-date information can be obtained from the social services' customer relations department or similar office in the local authority. Look for the telephone number under Social Services ('Social Work' in Scotland) or the Primary Care Trust (Local Health Board in Wales) or relevant Age Concern Factsheets.

Social services departments can charge recipients of services for many of their services, depending on personal circumstances. In some circumstances, they can also charge carers for carers' services. The local authority concerned has a legal duty to carry out an assessment, using a set of eligibility criteria, if the person may need community care services. The assessment should determine whether, and at what level, care might be needed. If the person needs residential or community care, the local authority must then pay for meeting any necessary care costs, at the agreed level, once a means test (an assessment of a person's financial circumstances – see page 118) has been carried out. The assessment looks at long term needs; however, there are provisions that allow authorities to make a reasonable charge for placements of less than five weeks.

After a needs assessment has been completed, the cost of any care services offered will be explained before a care plan (set of services) is agreed. The rates that apply under the charging procedure for residential care are set nationally by central government, and are subject to change. Charges for care within the person's own home are discretionary. The needs assessment and the financial assessment are undertaken separately and the results should have no bearing on each other. People who are eligible for payment of nursing care, if they have continuing physical or mental healthcare needs, are assessed against a set of established criteria.

For more information

ⓘ Age Concern Factsheet 10 *Local authority charging procedures for care homes.*

Social services

Alison, carers' support worker

'Carers are bombarded with information when they are desperate and least able to listen calmly – it is much better to take in small pieces of advice when it is most needed rather than try and remember everything at once.'

Local social services departments are the main agencies for co-ordinating the provision of community care services for older people. Not all people with poor memory function will require direct services from a social services department so skip over this section if you feel it does not apply to your relative's needs at present. The information will be helpful for some families at some times. In all areas close liaison takes place between community nurses and social workers, and care will be shared when necessary.

Social services assessments, care plans and eligibility criteria

Carers UK

'When carers have an assessment they get more services.'

Freda, carers' support worker

'Many services have been reduced in areas where budgets are tight. Carers must ask for a proper assessment, this is a legal right and is not affected by cutbacks.'

Social services departments are responsible for providing a wide range of home, residential and day care services. This is provided direct through their own home care service, or purchased for your relative from voluntary or commercial organisations (sometimes called the independent sector). Demand for services is heavy and most departments have limited financial resources so they apply strict eligibility criteria (tests) to decide which services to provide. These assessments, in some form, apply generally throughout the UK, though there are some local variations. However, they should all be in keeping with the guidance laid out by the Government in the document *Fair Access to Care Services*, published in 2001. The example of assessment given below is typical, although the availability of individual services will differ from area to area.

The Single Assessment Process (SAP)

'NHS and social care services treat older people as individuals and enable them to make choices about their own care. This is achieved through the Single Assessment Process, integrated commissioning arrangements, and integrated provision of services.'

Source: National Service Framework for Older People. Published by the Department of Health in 2001

The first stage of the *assessment* process is intended to gather basic information about the situation and the care needs. It will usually take place in an appropriate surrounding as a face-to-face meeting and time will be taken to answer your questions. However, certain details may be discussed beforehand by telephone to establish the urgency of the situation. At the end of the assessment the care needs of your relative are clearly defined and, if no further help and advice is needed, an agreement is reached with your relative (provided they are mentally capable) and you about what those care needs are. For the purpose of assessment these usually fall into five basic categories:

- **Physical safety.** The person has regular falls.
- **Physical disability.** Mobility, sight or hearing problems.
- **Mental health.** Severe memory loss or depression leading to neglect.

- **Loss of independent living skills.** Inability to cook, wash or dress themselves.
- **Social needs.** The person has become very isolated and lonely.

The assessor then decides the *level of need* from low to very high risk.

Once it is decided that a person is eligible to receive services, discussions take place between everyone immediately involved to devise a care plan that best suits the needs of the family. The eligibility criteria continue to apply if your relative is already receiving services. The needs of you both will be *re-assessed* by means of a *review*, and services may change as a result of this process. Again, everyone immediately concerned will be fully involved and informed of any decisions about future care. If you do not agree with the result of the assessment, you may appeal against it via the social services complaints procedure (a social worker or care manager will advise you about the process). Social services departments will investigate any complaint seriously and will suggest that you obtain independent advice. The local Citizens Advice Bureau may be able to advise you.

Home care (social services)

Help for adults with day to day care, living in their own homes, includes:

- personal care (eg washing, toileting, going to bed);
- practical help (eg housework or shopping) although this type of help is more likely to be provided by a separate agency;
- help for carers who may be partners, relatives or friends (eg respite care);
- advice and equipment from an occupational therapist (eg commodes, bed raisers);
- help for people with specialist needs from specialist staff (eg those with hearing or sight loss, or physical disabilities).

Care assistants give personal care, such as washing and toileting, and carry out basic treatments. They are not trained nurses so do not carry out elaborate nursing procedures.

Since April 2002, the way charges are calculated for home care in the different UK countries differ slightly. Guidelines giving the appropriate charging structures are available locally.

For more information

ⓘ Age Concern Factsheet 41 *Local Authority assessment for community care services.*

ⓘ Age Concern Factsheet 6 *Finding help at home.*

ⓘ Age Concern Factsheet 46 *Paying for care and support at home.*

Health care services (NHS)

Services from the NHS for people with health care needs includes the provision of general and specialist care, loan of equipment, rehabilitation, respite health care and continuing NHS care (ie, care the NHS pays for in full). This latter point can mean that the NHS pays the full fees for agreed nursing care. The main decisions about what health services will be provided for people locally are taken by Primary Care Trusts, which also commission services from other NHS Trusts and the independent sector, to complement their own provision. You can get information about health services from your GP surgery or health centres, or from NHS Direct. NHS and social services staff should work closely with your GP to maintain continuity of care.

Local health services tend to fall into three categories:

■ **Acute health care.** Given at NHS hospital trusts that offer specialist tests and treatments through inpatient and outpatient services.
■ **Community health care.** Provided by NHS Primary Care Trusts that offer day to day care from a range of services, including community psychiatric and general nursing, physiotherapy, occupational therapy and chiropody.
■ **Tertiary health care.** Provided by care homes.

Eligibility criteria for continuing NHS health care

Each Strategic Health Authority sets its eligibility criteria for these services based on national guidelines. They must be published and should be available from the local NHS body. Your relative's continuing health care needs will be assessed against these criteria. The 'eligibility' assessment process will be broached sensitively for patients with mental health problems. An NHS patient receiving treatment in hospital and requiring services after discharge will be assessed before leaving hospital.

If long term, hospital-based care is not needed, social services and NHS professionals will work together to prepare a care plan to be provided in the person's own home or in a care home. The care given to each patient is overseen by one senior person, who works with a small team of staff to ensure consistent care. The name given to this key person may vary from area to area, but it is designed to fulfil the same purpose – the role of care 'manager'.

The views and wishes of the person and their family are taken into account. If they do not agree with the decision to discharge the patient from hospital they can ask an independent review panel to look at the decision. If this applies to you, the Patient Advice and Liaison Service (PALS) in England, the Community Health Councils in Wales, the Mental Health Commission in Northern Ireland, the Health Council in Scotland or a leading mental health charity can help you if you are unsure how to proceed (see pages 91 and the Useful addresses list on pages 162–176).

Home care (NHS)

The Community Nursing Service operates throughout the country, providing general and psychiatric nursing treatment and care for people who remain at home. Community mental health and general nurses are often based at GP surgeries and health centres; patients are usually referred by their GPs but anyone can contact a community nurse direct. If a care plan has already been set up following hospital discharge, the appropriate community nurse will call automatically. But if your relative has not been discharged recently and you feel you need help or advice, you may telephone for an assessment. Don't wait until you are desperate, particularly if the state of your relative's memory function is failing quickly or they have become incontinent. Community nurses can provide a great deal of local information about resources and can put you in touch with other services and arrange equipment and items such as incontinence pads. Ask for a telephone number at your surgery or leave a message for the nurse.

Kathy, a carer

'I felt so relieved when the mental health nurse came to us. I wanted my husband to stay at home, so when his memory was getting weaker the nurse talked to me about how I could get the best response from him and helped me sort out the right times for all his pills.'

For more information

- 🛈 Age Concern Factsheet 32 *Disability and ageing: your rights to social services*.

- 🛈 Age Concern Factsheet 37 *Hospital discharge arrangements, and NHS continuing health care services*.

- 🛈 Age Concern Factsheet 20 NHS *Continuing Care, free nursing care and intermediate care*.

- 🛈 Age Concern Factsheet 44 *NHS services for older people*.

- 🛈 NHS Direct on 0845 4647, a 24-hour information and helpline available in England.

Pharmacists (chemists) and prescriptions

Pharmacists provide a number of services to the community and are a valuable source of information about medicines, 'over-the-counter' treatments (which don't need a prescription) and any minor health problems not serious enough to take to a surgery. Pharmacists will advise you to speak to the GP if they feel there is a need for medical treatment. Before you speak to a pharmacist, make a list of all medication your relative is taking, so that he or she can be sure that drugs will not interact with each other.

Pharmacists have particular responsibility for making up prescriptions for medicines or certain medical aids. You may take a prescription to any pharmacy but, for people living in rural areas, a dispensing service is available at surgeries and health centres if the nearest pharmacist/chemist shop is more than one mile away. Ask about the availability of this service if you are unsure. There is normally a charge for prescriptions, but certain groups of people qualify for free medication. Current exemptions are available for people on income support, people over retirement age, and people with certain illnesses such as diabetes, however, changes may be made to these categories under proposed future legislation. Having memory loss does not automatically mean that your relative will be exempt, unless they are past retirement age.

Pharmacists can help in other ways, such as supplying and/or filling a special box to help someone take the correct drug dose at the correct time of day, and putting medicines in non child-proof containers if a person has difficulty opening standard caps.

Pre-payment certificates are available to help spread the cost for people who need regular medication but do not qualify for free prescriptions.

For more information

ℹ Leaflet FP 95 *Prepayment of prescription charges*, available from the Health Benefits Division of the NHS, Tel: 0845 6018076.

ℹ Your local pharmacy, chemist or GP surgery should be able to help with any queries relating to medication or prescriptions.

Voluntary services

There is a wide range of voluntary organisations providing services, self-help and support to carers at national and regional levels. Some voluntary organisations provide services that are broadly targeted – for example the advice and information available from Citizens Advice Bureaux – while others offer help with specific diseases such as arthritis or depression. There are no charities dealing solely with the issue of memory loss, other than as a symptom of dementia, so for purposes of illustration in this book the term mental health charities might be used as the best sources of advice and support. Services provided by the voluntary sector may carry charges to cover costs.

Many voluntary sector organisations are directly contracted by the NHS and social services to provide care locally. The services are professionally managed by well trained staff; day centres for older patients, transport schemes and meals on wheels are good examples. National charities dealing with services for older people and carers offer support through telephone helplines, newsletters and self-help groups. Many also have local branches.

No two areas will offer identical services, so you will have to find out what you can expect to obtain in your part of the country. The two main sign-posting organisations for local voluntary sector services can be found in the telephone directory under Council for Voluntary Services (CVS) and Volunteer Bureau (or contact their national associations, see pages 171 and 176.

Specialist agencies

There are many organisations that work directly with and for older people with mental health problems – too many to cover fully here. The larger charities offer materials and advice covering all aspects of treatments and some provide direct 'hands-on' care. The smaller charities tend to offer a specialist service. Many charities also fund and undertake and/or support research into mental ill health. For contact details of the main charities see the Useful addresses list on page 162. Ask at your GP surgery or health centre about what is available in your local area. The full range of services, spread across several organisations, is very varied including:

■ written literature, eg leaflets, factsheets, books, newsletters;
■ audio and visual tapes for people with impaired senses, and the provision of clear, pictorial information for all patients and carers;
■ Internet access to website material, including texts similar to leaflets and fact sheets;
■ helpline services that enable patients and carers to speak directly to a trained nurse or counsellor;
■ access to urgent welfare items where there is a time delay or absence in statutory provision;
■ training programmes for doctors and nurses to improve the care and treatment of mental health patients and to help professional workers be better informed so that they can promote a greater understanding among the public.

The key charities are listed alphabetically in the address section at the end of the book. Contact their national offices for direct information or details of what facilities are available at regional centres.

Independent care providers

Help at home is available from private and voluntary agencies that offer a range of services, including personal and domestic care, respite facilities, holiday accommodation and companionship. One such organisation, Crossroads Care (see page 166), has schemes in most areas of the country. Charges made by private organisations vary and may be greater than the rates charged by social services. If you wish to obtain care from an independent agency for your relative, or to top up the amount of care they receive from the local authority, ask your social worker for details or look in *Yellow Pages*.

> ## Vera, a carer
>
> 'As my husband's health got worse, we made a family decision about what would be the best thing to do and we all wanted to keep him at home with us. Because of his failing memory we never left him alone in the house and got help from a private care agency to give me breaks when he needed more care.'

Care homes

> ## Walter, a carer
>
> 'My grandfather already had a poor memory before he went into a home and the staff treated him with good care. He had become agitated about coping at home and was very relieved when I broached the topic. We visited several homes before he said that he felt it was the right one for him.'

Care homes offer permanent accommodation to people who are unable to live independently in the community. Many homes also offer respite care facilities and temporary places.

The definition and availability of care changed under the terms of the Care Standards Act (England) 2000 and Regulations of Care (Scotland) 2001; new procedures started everywhere in 2002. All residential and nursing homes are now called 'care homes' with different categories of home available, depending on the types of care offered. Various combinations of care might be offered; for example:

- homes that offer personal care only;
- homes that offer additional nursing care;
- homes that offer personal and nursing care with the facility to provide medicines and medical treatments;
- homes that also cater for people with dementia and those who are terminally ill.

126

Your relative can purchase all their care needs from private agencies (if they are willing to pay the charge) or, in a few specific instances, if their local authority agrees to give them 'direct payments' to pay directly for the social services that they have been assessed as needing. The provision that nursing care is free in any setting in England since October 2001, and nursing and personal care costs are free in Scotland, since April 2002, still applies.

At the outset of caring you and your relative may be coping well and may not wish to consider these as an option. However, over a period of time, if the care situation becomes stressful or your relative's health deteriorates, moving to a home may become the best or only choice open to you both. In such a situation, it is vital that everyone involved in the decision has a chance to express their feelings about seeking permanent care, provided they are mentally capable. If your relative is able, you should discuss with them the merits of staying at home or entering a care home, and weigh up the possible advantages and disadvantages for everyone concerned. Think about all the factors that might influence the decision. For example:

- The benefit of increased safety and care provided by trained staff.
- Peace of mind and less stress for the carer, especially if relationships have become strained.
- Ready made companionship – but loss of privacy and independence.
- Feelings of guilt and the loss of a close relative from the immediate family circle.
- The costs of travel and time.
- The difficulty finding a suitable care home.
- The overall cost of care homes set against charges for care at home.
- Could your relative continue to live at home or in 'extra care' housing if the level of services were increased?

Taking the discussion a stage further

It is not easy to decide which type of home to live in and the decision should not be made hurriedly. A list of addresses can be obtained from the local authority, and details can then be obtained direct from individual care homes. Some residential-type homes (whether run by statutory bodies, voluntary organisations or the independent sector) offer living accommodation but do not provide nursing care, so it could be worth considering a home that provides more comprehensive care if you believe that your relative might come to need specialist attention. All types of care homes make charges according to a financial assessment (see page 115), unless your relative has chosen to make their own private contract with the home and pay the full fees. Even if this is the case you are both still entitled to an assessment from social services.

Ask around among your friends and acquaintances about the care homes you are considering. Word of mouth is a useful source of information and gives a measure of local feeling about the facilities offered. When you and your relative are getting closer to making a decision, gather together details, draw up a short list and arrange to visit the homes. It is important to 'get a feel' for the atmosphere and care provided. If possible, see if you and your relative can visit to share a meal or other activities with current residents. You might want to ask yourselves some questions to help assess what type of home would be best.

■ How mobile is your relative?
■ What is his/her current physical and mental state and is this likely to change rapidly?
■ Is your relative now so vague and forgetful that they can no longer cope independently?
■ How much care and supervision is needed – round the clock cover or day time support only?
■ What type of care is needed – protection and security, nursing care including medication and treatments or personal hygiene care only?
■ Will special aids and equipment be needed?

Remember also the things that your relative likes to do or feels are important. Many activities can still bring pleasure to them even if their memory is less reliable. For example, if being able to attend a church, enjoy a favourite meal, have regular visitors or walk in the fresh air matter (or have done in the past) it is important that they will have the opportunity to continue with these activities.

Registration and inspection

All care homes, whether independent or statutory, are subject to standard registration and inspection procedures, carried out locally. All inspection reports must be publicly available. You can find out more about registration criteria by contacting the local department (contact details will be available at your social services office). Some independent agencies belong to organisations that require them to meet their own independent standards, such as those set by the United Kingdom Home Care Association (UKHCA), in addition to the national criteria set by the Care Standards Act.

Making a complaint

If you are not happy with the services you receive from any organisation (NHS, social services or voluntary agencies) you should try to resolve the situation as soon as possible by speaking to the person involved. This could be the senior person on duty, your care manager or home manager. If you are still not satisfied and wish to take the matter further, contact a customer relations department or equivalent (a voluntary organisation will have a management committee) and ask for details of their complaints procedure. Most NHS Trusts now have a PALS (Patient Advice and Liaison Services) Manager who will be able to help you make a complaint. For independent help about how to deal with a complaints procedure, contact your local Citizens Advice Bureau. Alternatively, Age Concern runs an Advocacy Service for people over the age of 65 in some areas.

For more information

i Carers Handbook Series *Finding and paying for residential and nursing home care*. Marina Lewycka, published by Age Concern Books. (Currently out of print, but might be available through public libraries.)

i Age Concern Factsheet 6 *Finding help at home*.

i Age Concern Factsheet 20 *NHS continuing care, free nursing care and intermediate care*.

ⓘ Age Concern Factsheet 29 *Finding care home accommodation.*

ⓘ Age Concern Factsheet 39 P*aying for care in a care home if you have a partner.*

ⓘ Age Concern Factsheet 40 *Transfer of assets and paying for care in a care home.*

ⓘ Elderly Accommodation Counsel, provides a national register of accommodation in the voluntary and private sectors suitable for older people (see page 168).

ⓘ Independent Healthcare Association is a representative and lobbying organisation for private care homes (see page 170).

ⓘ Jewish Care, provides a wide range of social services for the Jewish community, particularly elderly people (see page 170).

ⓘ Relatives and Residents Association, provides advice for the relatives of people in a care home or in hospital long-term (see page 173).

ⓘ United Kingdom Homecare Association, represents the interests of home care organisations and promotes standards of care. UK helpline provides information on agencies working to the agreed code of practice (see page 175).

ⓘ For registration and inspection units, look in the local telephone directory, or ask at your social services department or health authority.

Facilities that support home care

Respite care

Jack, a carer

'I had arranged a break in advance through the social worker and when the time came I knew I was ready. I went to my daughter for a week and my wife went into temporary accommodation. We did miss each other but having to keep repeating myself because she asked the same questions again and again had got a bit wearing. Afterwards I felt ready to carry on again.'

Hassan, Community mental health nurse

'I specialise in working with older people and many of my patients have problems with short term memory loss which can be quite frustrating for their relatives. I meet many carers who are desperate for a rest so I am happy to help them arrange respite breaks. I emphasise that time out is essential for their own health and well-being and will help them to cope better. If they start to disagree, I point out that their relative might also welcome a break from the usual routine.'

All carers need a break from caring, to be alone or to spend time with other family members and friends away from the caring situation. This type of break is called 'respite care' and can take many forms, for example:

■ a couple of hours out to do some shopping, read a magazine or visit a friend;
■ a longer period to take a weekend break or a holiday;
■ time spent at home catching up on jobs while your relative goes to a day centre;
■ an uninterrupted night's sleep.

Breaks like these are not a luxury. Everyone needs to take time out to 'recharge' their energy and reduce the stressed load. The Government NHS Plan recognises the importance of respite care in its Better Care – Higher Standards Charter, which indicates that information about 'types of breaks for carers' must be available locally. Even if you feel fine at present, try not to leave it until you are desperate for a break before attempting to make arrangements. Respite care can always be organised if there is an emergency, but it is much better to have a regular time set aside, for several reasons: the agencies which organise the respite care need sufficient planning time, bed space is limited for this type of care and it enables you to plan ahead and have something to look forward to. The effort needed to organise a break may be more than you feel you can take on if you are at crisis point. You might be doubtful about handing your relative over to someone else, even for an hour or so, but the break should be good for both of you. Try to involve your relative in making plans, if at all possible. For example, if there is more than one option, your relative might want to make the choice.

A social worker or community psychiatric nurse would explain about how carers can be assessed for provision of services and can help you make arrangements. Or you can contact the national agencies listed below.

■ **British Nursing Association** This agency provides care assistants, home helps and qualified nurses to care for individual people in their own homes. A wide range of services are offered including convalescent care, night care, personal care, shopping, companionship and respite care. The organisation caters for every level of need from occasional visits to live-in care. Look in the telephone directory for a local number or contact.

■ **Crossroads Care Schemes** The local schemes are part of a national network set up to provide practical help and support to older people, disabled people and their carers. Each situation is assessed individually with the trained care attendant taking over the role of the family carer. Using the Crossroads Scheme will give you an opportunity for a respite break at a time of your choosing; care is given 365 days of the year. See page 166 for the address, or look in the telephone directory for a local number.

Charges are usually made for respite care. Each organisation will give you details relating to your relative's circumstances. If regular respite care is part of your relative's care from social services, ask them what charges (if any) there might be. People who meet their health authority's criteria for NHS respite health care may have this provided (free of charge) in a hospital or hospice.

Day care

Vera, a carer

'The ambulance came on Thursdays to take Robert to the day centre. He would have rather stayed at home some weeks, but he realised that I needed to have a rest. Sometimes a friend came for a cup of tea or I did things such as going to the dentist. The social worker set it up for us.'

Day care for your relative is another way for you to have time to yourself, and for your relative to enjoy activities and different company away from their home routine. All local authorities and many voluntary organisations provide day care facilities at specialist (eg for people with dementia) and non-specialist day centres offering a range of social activities and levels of care. Lunch is always provided and, depending on local facilities, your relative might have access to chiropody, hair dressing, complementary therapies, even a bath if this is difficult at home. Or they can sit quietly and rest.

Some services operate in purpose built day centres, while others share accommodation in community centres and residential homes. The staff are trained, professional workers with additional volunteer help in many centres. For more details ask your social worker or community psychiatric nurse.

Continence and laundry services

Rachael, a carer

'The community nurse said that my mother was eligible for incontinence pads and the boxes arrived at the door. We didn't get as many as we would have liked so we only used the pads at night but they made such a difference. I had less washing and we both slept better because she stopped calling me or worrying about wetting the bed.'

If your relative is incontinent, excellent help can be found in most areas through the Continence Advisory Service. Ask at your GP surgery for details. A community nurse or continence adviser will make an assessment. Incontinence has many causes, and it may be possible to improve the symptoms considerably with treatment.

For people who have heavy urine and soiling problems, incontinence pads are available and it may be possible to make use of a home collection laundry service. Facilities vary around the country. Incontinence supplies are free from the NHS, however, the quantity of pads supplied may be limited.

For more information

ℹ Age Concern Factsheet 23 *Help with incontinence.*

Meals on wheels

A meals service is provided for older or disabled persons in all areas. It is run by the Women's Royal Voluntary Service or other local organisations, and these reasonably priced meals are delivered either hot daily or as a pre-packed frozen service at regular intervals. A choice of type is not always available. Referral is via a healthcare professional or the social services.

Extra equipment

Caring for someone at home is likely to become more difficult as the person becomes less mobile. Mobility tends to decline gradually if health and strength fails – unlike the abruptness of paralysis immediately following a stroke for example. So, for you and your relative, each stage can be assessed regularly and you can adjust to whatever degree of movement remains. Aids and equipment to help with moving and handling patients are used frequently by professional carers nowadays as part of Health and Safety regulations. Many useful pieces of equipment can be hired or loaned free of charge from social services, NHS trusts and voluntary organisations.

- **Wheelchair** This is essential for mobility inside and outside the house, especially if your relative has trouble breathing and finds it an effort to walk even short distances.

- **Urine bottle/bedpan** Nowadays many people prefer to purchase these items from a pharmacy or chemist, but bedpans can be borrowed or hired if necessary.

- **Commode** This piece of 'furniture' is necessary in the later stages of an illness but can be useful if your relative needs to use the toilet during the night.

- **Sliding sheets** Made of a slippery nylon fabric, the two surfaces slide easily when placed together to move a person in any direction on chairs, beds and car seats.

- **Moving aids (hand held)** These firm, flat plastic supports can be placed under the thighs or the back of an individual and held by two people to make movement in a bed or chair easier. Alternatively, a banana-shaped board can be placed between a chair and the bed (or wheelchair) to slide the person across so that they do not have to be raised into a standing position. Using aids such as these puts less strain on frail limbs and shoulder joints – for both the patient and their carers.

- **Mechanical hoist** These operate by electric or hydraulic power and are used mainly in care home settings by professional carers for people who are very difficult to move. Hoists can also be recommended for use in the home, after assessment.

- **Bed and chair raisers** These look like heavy-duty, plastic flowerpots and are excellent for raising furniture by several inches to ease the strain of bending and moving.

- **Special mattresses** Several types are available to help protect vulnerable pressure points when a person becomes chair-bound or bed-ridden.

- **Pillow support or back rest** Again, several types are available.

- **Handrails and ramps** These can be positioned at various places, such as the bathroom and at the entrance to the house.

- **Bath aids** Bath aids range from basic non-slip mats to mechanical lifts.

- **Adapted crockery and cutlery** These can be used for general eating and drinking, or for kitchen use if your relative enjoys helping with the cooking or wants to make a hot drink.
- **Two-way 'listening' system, mobile telephone, answering machine or entryphone** All of these offer a means of communication without the need to rush, climb stairs unnecessarily or even be in the same building.
- **Personal alarms** See emergency help systems (page 160).

Jack, a carer

'I hired a commode and it made such a difference. It had wheels so I pushed it right over the toilet seat (without the pot during the day and used the pot at night). My wife was unsure at first and kept asking why it was in the bedroom but it soon became part of the furniture.'

In all areas of the country, your first point of call for information about equipment loans will be through a community nurse or occupational therapist (OT). An assessment of your relative's needs will be arranged. Occupational therapists work towards restoring and maintaining levels of independence and reducing the impact of illness. They may be based with social services or the NHS depending whether your relative has been referred to them because of a health or a social need. Ask the community nurse or your doctor to make a referral for a home visit if you are unsure which agency to approach. Equipment supplied by the NHS is lent free of charge. Unfortunately, waiting lists for certain pieces of equipment are long in many areas.

For more information

- Age Concern Factsheet 42 *Disability equipment and how to get it.*
- The Disabled Living Foundation offers advice on aids and equipment (see page 168).

ℹ️ Disabled Living Centres Council (see page 166) can tell you the centre nearest you, where you can see and try out aids and equipment.

ℹ️ The local branches of the British Red Cross or St John Ambulance give advice and arrange the hire or loan of equipment. Look in the telephone directory for a contact number or ask the district nurse for a referral.

ℹ️ Many pharmacist/chemist shops sell aids and small pieces of equipment or keep catalogues for mail order.

ℹ️ Care and Repair UK provides advice and practical help to older and disabled people and those on low incomes, to help them improve their home conditions. Charges are made, but these can be set against a grant if one is provided (see page 165).

Conclusion

The decision whether to look after your relative at home or arrange care in a care home will be based on a number of factors: the wishes of the person concerned; your ability to give quality care; the support that other family members can give; and the type and amount of care that is needed. It is not an easy decision and cannot be taken lightly, especially if the move is liable to disturb your relative's failing memory yet more. Caring for someone else is a time-consuming and strenuous occupation that draws heavily on the personal resources of the main carer. This task is almost impossible to undertake single handed and relies on the support of the professional services as well as family and friends. If the care is long term, it can put a strain on relationships and stretch finances.

Whatever your initial decision may be, it is important that you review this from time to time and accept that no carer can ever make a promise that is binding forever.

The final chapter looks carefully at what it means to be a carer, a role which many people feel ill-equipped to take on when they first assume responsibility for another person.

8 The caring role

The term 'carer' is used to mean anyone who spends time and energy looking after someone in need of extra attention because of their age or physical or other disability. This could be a friend or neighbour, but is most likely to be a close relative. The word 'carer' in this context is intended to denote an 'informal' or 'non-professional' person, rather than a trained worker. This chapter offers support and guidance to help you in your role of carer.

Becoming a carer may lay you open to some strong, and perhaps confusing, feelings and it may take a while for you to adjust. Taking on a caring role, particularly where this involves caring for someone you love dearly, is not something you set out to do, like a professional job with ample training. Families enter into a caring relationship in one of a number of ways: perhaps very swiftly, following the dramatic diagnosis of an acute illness or a stroke; more gradually, as the health of a relative with an existing illness deteriorates; or simply because their relative can no longer manage alone. Your relative's memory function is obviously causing concern – in addition you may have other underlying reasons for your taking on this role.

It could be argued that this chapter should have come earlier, in recognition of the fact that dealing with someone with severe memory loss can be quite harrowing. Its inclusion here at the end of the book is not intended as an afterthought or to pay lip-service to your caring role; instead, view its position more as a reassurance about some of the issues related to being a carer, and as a final token of support.

What does it mean to be a carer?

In general terms, caring varies from a full-time activity if someone is seriously ill to as little as keeping a regular eye on a relative's daily affairs. The aim of most carers is to help the less able person to remain in their own home, leading as stress free and independent a life as possible, for as long as they can. Fact Box 2 gives some figures to show that you are not alone in your situation. Wherever your position on the spectrum of care – from very part-time to very full-time – it is likely you are fulfilling a number of the following commitments:

- providing a safe and comfortable home;
- doing practical jobs such as shopping, cooking, cleaning, laundry and gardening;
- giving personal care and carrying out basic nursing procedures;
- offering love, emotional support and company;
- bringing a bit of the 'outside world' into the daily life of someone who may otherwise be quite isolated;
- providing help and advice on running personal affairs.

Fact Box 2

1 Over six million people in the UK look after a relative or friend who cannot manage without help because of illness, frailty or disability.

2 Ten per cent of the total population, or about 12 per cent of the adult population have a caring role.

3 More women (3.9 million, 18 per cent) than men (2.9 million, 14 per cent) are carers.

---

4   The peak age for becoming a carer is between 45 to 64 years (25 per cent of adults in this age group).

5   Estimates suggest there may be 51,000 carers aged 16 years or under – most of them care for a parent.

6   The financial costs of caring are significant and the support is paltry. Carers' Allowance (available to certain carers) is one of the lowest welfare benefits of its kind.

7   Seventy-seven per cent of carers who responded to a survey by Carers UK claimed to be financially 'worse off'.

8   Six out of ten carers felt it was affecting their own health. A further study found that over 20 per cent of carers providing over 20 hours of care a week had a mental health problem themselves.

9   CarersLine (see page 165) receives over 20,000 enquiries per year.

Source: *Facts About Carers*, Published May 2003, by Carers UK

Recognising yourself as a carer

Vera, a carer

'When Robert began to forget things badly I felt so scared and was shocked when a doctor said it would probably get worse – I couldn't think about what to do next. When he first needed more help I never called myself a carer.'

You may not think of yourself as a carer because you undertake your tasks out of love and friendship, and you may have fallen into the caring role because no-one else is available. Many carers do not recognise themselves as such and therefore do not seek information or know where to look for further help. Now that your relative has a failing memory it is vital that you are aware of the support and help that is available and that, as a carer, you also have rights that go alongside the responsibilities. This chapter offers information, advice and support to anyone who cares in some way for a spouse, relative or friend. It cannot give you all the answers or solve all your problems, but it may help you better to understand some of the issues faced by non-professional carers.

Warren, needs regular care

'My daughter comes to see me every other day. She lives in the next village and pops by on her way home. I know I forget things so it's a relief that she sorts out my paperwork and does most of my shopping. It's a strange feeling not being able to remember whether you've done something or not.'

There are an estimated six million carers in the UK (around one in eight people), nearly two million of whom provide substantial amounts of care. However, published figures do vary according to the source of the information. Mostly, numbers are taken from two major (government run) surveys: the General Household Survey (GHS) and the National Census (NC), with the GHS sometimes giving higher numbers. Carers UK say that the GHS is a more detailed survey, compiled using data from face-to-face interviews, whilst the NC relies on people completing a form independently. The GHS probably picks up on more people because they identify them selves as carers when asked.

At times, being a carer creates tremendous anxiety and distress; you may be undertaking tasks that feel difficult and unfamiliar, you are largely unpaid and untrained, and are often on duty for 24 hours each day, seven days a week. You will need to pace yourself, use a range of skills and experience, take on an enduring commitment, build up strong physical and mental systems, control your emotions and maintain a good sense of humour. Quite a lot to expect from one untrained person! This responsibility will tax your patience and you won't always get it right. Life is never completely straightforward and you may feel that it has already dealt you a nasty blow. But there are many sources of help and support you can draw upon to help you cope with very difficult situations and find ways of managing the stress.

Your perceptions and feelings as a carer

Freda works as a carers' support worker

'Carers often feel tired and upset – these are normal reactions to the situation. But if you begin to feel over-stressed, angry and weepy, these powerful emotions may be a signal that you need a short break. I realise it's easy to say "be calm", but lots of emotional energy can be spent worrying when it won't actually help.'

You will have your ups and downs and there will be days when you feel you cannot cope. Even if you chose your caring situation without hesitation, this will not stop you from having negative feelings; and while many people decide to care willingly this will not be true of every carer. Professional people who work with carers understand that carers feel a range of very conflicting emotions, and that sometimes these will spill over and be directed both towards their relative and towards the people who offer them support. Anger, frustration, fear, resentment and guilt will often exist alongside other emotions such as sadness, love, anxiety and concern. Powerful emotions can drain and exhaust you, so try not to add 'worry' to the list. Worry and guilt are two emotions that cause much wasted energy. Look instead at problems from a different angle: if you feel in control, you will cope well; if the problem is not within your control, spending time being worried or guilty won't improve the situation and may even prevent you from finding a solution. Carers frequently bottle up strong emotions to protect others, but everyone needs an outlet for themselves. Letting go of unhappy feelings is better than storing them up.

Kathy, a carer

'I sometimes felt angry with Dick, wondering why he couldn't remember. The doctor explained it was the strokes but when he forgot where he had put his glasses yet again, I had to control my emotions. This was my strong husband needing so much support.'

Sizing up the problem

It is still assumed in society today that a blood-tie or marriage relationship automatically makes a person (usually the woman in the partnership) the main carer and that, in this role, she or he must undertake a number of onerous, unpaid tasks. You may believe this yourself. It may be assumed by others that you have the ability to cope and that your capacity to care can stretch to meet all the demands that are placed upon you. You may feel that other people expect so much from you – family members, doctors, social workers and nurses – and that you cannot let them down.

To help you come to terms with your role of carer, it is important that you think about all of these expectations, including what you expect of yourself. If you feel confused or overwhelmed by the enormity of the task, talking to someone – perhaps another carer or a counsellor – might help (see below). Look at the list below and tick off those feelings that have crossed your mind in recent weeks.

■ I lack confidence and feel inadequate.
■ I have no qualifications to do the job.
■ I am worried about shortage of money.
■ I lack recognition/status.
■ I am not sure where to turn for allies or support.
■ I am bewildered by the maze of services.
■ I am unclear about what I can ask for.
■ I feel the 'patient's' needs are always given precedence over mine.
■ I have no time or space to be myself.
■ I feel that no one cares for me.

These thoughts are very common, even if they have been only fleeting. Don't block them out. Accept that occasionally carers do feel unable to carry on; that carers themselves may become depressed if they overdo it, and sometimes they feel forced to take dramatic steps to make their voice heard. Support workers will endeavour to ease your position and avert a crisis; however, although risks can be minimised, a crisis can never be ruled out totally. Unfortunately, not all carers have access to an adequate, informal support system. If this applies to you, do speak to your GP or the duty Social Worker at your closest social services office and ask about additional help before crisis point is reached.

Setting boundaries

Alison, a carers' support worker

'Many people become carers without being aware that carers have rights to services and that they do have choices about their situation. There should be a Government health warning – "Caring can seriously damage your health"!'

How did you become a carer? Did it creep up on you slowly as your relative's memory loss got worse, or were you thrust into the role suddenly because of a crisis? Whatever the original reason it is vital that, at some point, you sit back and take stock of the current situation. Ask yourself a few searching questions and think logically and seriously about the answers. Perhaps an unbiased listener will help you sort out your feelings? An appointment with a counsellor can often be arranged through your GP surgery or health centre. Alternatively, you can phone a helpline and talk to a counsellor. You can use CarersLine on 0808 808 7777 or a mental health charity (see the Useful addresses list on page 162).

Ask yourself the following questions:

- Why am I doing this job?
- Will I feel I have rejected someone I love if I stop?
- Is the caring situation going to be long term or short term?
- Are other people pressuring me to continue?
- Do I want to carry on or pass the responsibility over to others?
- What are my options for change?

As a carer you must make a conscious decision about whether to continue with caring or not, because making a definite choice will increase your mental strength to cope with the task – however difficult it might be. There may be times when carers feel in despair, but when they perceive that they have no choice, that they were forced into the situation by others or that they did not fully consider the seriousness of the situation before it overtook them, they are more likely to become angry, resentful and suffer ill health. There is nothing wrong with saying 'no' if you already feel over burdened. If you cannot continue to care for your relative at home, you can still continue to be involved with their day to day care.

How 'good' is your caring situation?

Paula, a carer

'As my mother's memory got worse I took over more of the responsibility for her day to day care. I lived around the corner so it was easy to stop by to and from work. We took each stage at a time and on her good days my mother and I talked honestly about how things were going.'

Researchers studying informal caring, given by close relatives, have identified a model of a *good* caring situation that is recognised by professional people as an important factor in maintaining a positive experience for the key people involved. While acknowledging that no caring situation can hope to fulfil the ideal all of the time, it is important that everyone accepts the value of such a model and works towards achieving *some* of the suggestions.

The list below can be seen as a 'model list' for a caring situation:

- The carer makes a conscious choice whether to care or not to care.
- The carer is able to recognise their own limits and needs.
- The carer lives close by, but not necessarily in the same house.
- A network of care is set up, so that responsibility is shared.
- Carers have time to themselves and don't have to give up most of their own life.
- Carers have access to information and help to learn skills.
- A good past relationship existed between the carer and the person being cared for.
- The dependent person wishes to stay as independent as possible.
- The dependent person retains their own friends.
- The carer fosters independence in the dependent person.
- Everybody keeps a sense of humour.
- Professional help is there when it is needed.
- The carer feels supported and valued.

Caring specifically for someone with memory loss

Rachael, a carer

'As my mother's memory problems got worse, I stopped trying to correct her or remind her that I knew already. I decided that it was pointless and frustrating — however, I did butt in when she was confusing other people, especially when it was clear that they were unsure how to handle the situation.'

'As my grandfather's memory problems got worse I began to choose my words very carefully as I knew that certain phrases would set him off on a story line that I had heard many times before. If I knew he enjoyed the tale or I had plenty of time I tried to say the right things but it did stretch my patience a bit.'

Living with (or supporting) someone who continually forgets even the most basic facts can be even more taxing than helping someone over a physical illness. However much you all love each other, a person who repeats stories over and over or leaves the gas fire on all night can cause deep feelings of frustration and irritation within the family, especially when practical efforts and physical love are insufficient tools to resolve the situation. And you, the main carer, may be at the centre of this turmoil. Don't be upset if this frustration then turns to guilt at the thought of being angry with someone who is clearly not in full control of their faculties. Families often express powerlessness at their inability to help lift the clouds and are fearful of what the outcome might be. Some relatives are also concerned for their own mental health, living in close proximity to so much negativity. Next time you forget a name you may even begin to wonder whether memory loss might be catching.

The simple answer to this question is 'No'. Memory dysfunction is not actually passed on from one person to another in the way that an infectious disease can be 'caught', although a worsening of the problem may influence the mood of others. If there is a history of noticeable memory loss running through a family, however, relatives should be aware of their own vulnerability and take some self-help measures. If you are affected mentally by dealing with your relative, you should take medical advice.

Despite worries about how useful they can be, the family and friends of a person with memory loss can play a significant role in helping them cope. Here are a few tips to help you gauge your level of response:

- Be a good listener. Never under estimate the value of being around to listen (positively). You can do this by acknowledging your relative's condition and encourage them to make the best of their residual memory.
- If your relative is prone to negative behaviour, give them a sense that you are sharing their worries without sharing their bleak view of their health and the future. It is also important that you protect yourself so, in your mind, set a time limit for discussing their feelings and then quietly but persistently edge the conversation towards more general matters. If your relative seems to be overly depressed, you should seek advice from the doctor.
- Spend some extra time with your relative, boost their confidence and make them feel special. Try to set some goals that are specific and realistic. You could write these down and go back to them after a week or so and review how well they have managed.
- Don't use bullying tactics even though you may feel frustrated by their possible lack of progress. A calm, firm manner is better, both for you and for them, otherwise you could both end up feeling upset.
- Do be open and honest – as most people, whatever their problem, appreciate directness and frankness. They will certainly not wish to feel that everyone is treating them with suspicion or keeping secrets.
- Reassure them and, although it is unlikely that their condition is treatable, in some way try to put their feelings into perspective and reduce any sense of isolation they might be feeling.
- Be prepared to repeat your tactics over and over again, as it is likely that they will be easily swayed by internal worry and doubt.
- In practical terms, make sure your relative is eating sufficient food, taking care of personal hygiene and not running too many risks.
- Conversely, don't be over protective because dissuading someone from taking risks can dampen their self-confidence.
- Never make promises – you do not know what the future will hold. A broken promise will make you both feel worse. (This rule applies especially to death-bed promises where you, the surviving person, may feel huge guilt at not fulfilling your relative's request).

148

What formal support is available for carers?

Increasingly, the rights and needs of carers are being taken into account, although it has taken many years of lobbying by pressure groups and individuals to introduce the changes in legislation we have now arrived at. A number of Acts of Parliament have been passed, and local charters produced, to secure and highlight the rights of carers and disabled people. The most relevant pieces of legislation are summarised here. If you need a more detailed explanation of the rights and services to which you are entitled, you should contact your local social services department (social work department in Scotland) which will be listed in the telephone directory.

State provision

NHS and Community Care Act 1990

The NHS and Community Care Act is designed to help meet the care needs of older people, those with learning and physical disabilities and mental health problems, preferably in their own home or the area where they live. Social services take the lead role and work together with the NHS and voluntary organisations to offer a broad range of services for people in need and their carers. The services cannot promise to meet all needs, because community care is subject to certain eligibility criteria (see pages 116 and 151). However a trained person, called a care manager, will assess the needs of the person you care for and then, if that person is eligible, arrange appropriate services in what is known as a 'care package'. The services (care package) arranged through social services are means-tested.

Carers (Recognition and Services) Act 1995

This Act came into force on 1st April 1996. It defines a carer as 'someone who provides (or intends to provide) a substantial amount of care on a regular basis', including care for children and young people under the age of 18 years. It contains two main elements that deal with the

149

rights of carers: to ask for a separate assessment of their care needs when the person they care for is being assessed or reassessed; and the duty of local authorities to take into consideration the findings of this assessment when deciding which services to offer the person being cared for (see Chapter 5).

The Act requires social services departments, if requested to do so by a carer, to assess the ability of a carer to provide and/or to continue to provide care, and take this care into account when deciding what services to provide to the person being cared for. To qualify for an assessment, a carer must be providing (or intending to provide) regular and substantial care, and the person they care for must be being assessed by social services at the same time. Because there is no official definition of 'regular' and 'substantial', each caring situation will be assessed individually. The assessment should recognise the carer's knowledge of the person, and the responsibility for the caring situation should be agreed as a shared undertaking between the carer and the social services department.

Carers UK

'The Carers (Recognition and Services) Act 1995, has been one of the most significant developments in the history of the carers' movement. Not only did it recognise the rights of carers for the first time, but the campaign which led to the Carers Act showed the level of agreement there was about the rights and needs of carers.'

Charters

Most social services departments have published charters in recent years, which aim to tell people what they can expect from the agencies that provide 'community care' services for adults. Two typical charters are summarised below. Contact your social services office to enquire about local versions.

150

Charters for carers

These charters usually acknowledge the valuable role carers perform in caring for someone at home. They state that practical help is a key priority for social services departments and set out how the department aims to respond to typical requests expressed by carers. The charters offer:

- opportunities for sharing experiences;
- recognition for carers;
- practical help;
- information and advice;
- advice about welfare benefits;
- a short break from caring.

Community care charters

These charters are concerned with the services that help people to remain in their own homes. They cover:

- being able to get in touch with the appropriate person;
- understanding people's needs;
- planning care;
- unmet needs;
- the services people can expect to receive;
- how to access information;
- what to do if things go wrong;
- relationships with people receiving services.

Both types of charter will be concerned with telling people about the services they can expect to receive for home care, personal help and care in care homes and how they can gain access to services more easily. Older people will also be represented on the independent, statutory Patients' Forum, set up from 2002 in every health trust area, so patients can have their say about how local NHS services are run.

Tracey, social worker

'As a professional person working directly with families of older people I acknowledge and respect the fact that not everyone is cut out to be a "carer". I meet many families who express feelings of limitation and I support them to find an alternative solution.'

Carers' support centres and workers

Alison, a carers' support worker

'Before you meet a professional person, jot down a few notes as it's important to ask the questions that are right for you. Try not to make assumptions about what you think may be available – people are often surprised at the amount of services that exist.'

There are many schemes set up around the country specifically to provide help and support for carers. They are run mainly by health and social services teams and voluntary organisations. The workers understand the problems and feelings of isolation experienced by carers and are specially trained to help carers receive relevant and up to date information, gain access to services and welfare benefits and guide them in their caring role. Support workers welcome contact with you as a carer and will listen to your hopes, concerns and fears. Many produce newsletters, run local support groups for carers and have drop-in and respite care facilities.

Freda, a carers' support worker

'We understand that carers get to the end of their tether and may be quite close to physical and mental collapse at times; occasionally it is their relative who takes the brunt of their anxieties and anger. Tension is usually relieved through shouting, but carers can lose their temper more violently. If you feel it's time to look at ways of relieving the strain then do seek help before you reach crisis point. If you feel really desperate then give the Samaritans a call.'

Your own needs as a carer

Kathy, a carer

'Although my husband's needs come first I do think about myself as well. If I couldn't function he would suffer so I try to rest when he is asleep and I sit with him and we listen to the radio together.'

Don't ignore your own health and well-being. This may sound like a tall order but you do need to maintain your own strength.

- Eat regularly and properly – if you are preparing meals for someone else try not to skimp on your own food.
- Take regular breaks from caring, even if you only find time to walk in the garden or read a book. Plan longer breaks at regular intervals.
- Arrange time away from the house to meet other people because isolation can be a major problem for many carers. There are sitting services available that will send a volunteer to stay with your relative – try your Age Concern locally or the local branch of the charity Crossroads (see page 166).
- Learn to move your relative safely, because strained and injured backs are a great problem for people who are suddenly thrust into a caring role. Ask your community nurse or social worker about how to do this.
- Take cat naps during the day if your night time sleep is disturbed. And don't feel guilty!
- Ask about help with housework or gardening if you are over tired. Some local councils and voluntary organisations run volunteer gardening schemes.

Talking about feelings

One of the difficulties faced by carers is how to talk to a relative about their memory loss. Likewise, the problem of how to tell other people may also be bothering them. In truth, any problem that has a mental health connection remains a topic that many people find awkward to broach and have difficulty discussing. There seems to be a 'code' that governs where and when sensitive subjects are introduced – for example, not in front of the person with the illness, nor within earshot of younger children. Carers and patients often find it easier to talk about their failing memory with professional people than with members of their own family; however, even doctors and nurses are not always comfortable answering questions and giving information. If this is creating difficulties for your relative and your family, try to persuade them that it is usually easier when the 'honesty' line is taken. A brief explanation, such as 'My mother's memory is not as good as it used to be', should suffice for adults.

Talking to children

Jodi, carer

'When Grandpa came to stay with us it was obvious to our younger children that he was acting strangely so my husband and I told Jon and Eva as plainly as we could about his difficulty in remembering things. We suggested ways that they might help him and that it was OK to come and chat to us about anything that felt weird. We also tried to make them understand that it was all right to laugh with him about the silly things he said occasionally but not fair to giggle in front of him too often.'

Talking to children about the health matters of a close relative will be a task that one family member must be prepared to take on. Children are often very perceptive and quick to pick up on family problems. However distressing it may be, it is better for children to be told at an early stage and then kept informed. Ask a health professional for help if this would make the job easier as they can advise you about how best to introduce the subject in an appropriate way. Talk to each child at a level that is right for their own emotional development, which may differ from that of other children in a peer or family group. Anyone given the responsibility of speaking to children should know them well because it is important to be aware of their reaction. It is also important to answer children's questions truthfully and simply, avoiding euphemisms which may be misunderstood. Even very young children will be aware if a parent, grandparent or close family member has an obvious problem with their memory, and will worry or be confused if no explanation is given. Children need to know how the person's actions will affect their own life and routine, and where possible their life should be disrupted as little as possible. It may be necessary to repeat the information several times and be prepared to return to subject as often as the child wishes, however upsetting this may feel for the adult.

Children have a right to be treated with respect and to be covered by the same code of confidentiality afforded to adults. Members of the wider family should be aware of what each child knows as children may approach others for confirmation. It is not fair to give a child false hope or inaccurate information to save an adult distress, so the information given should be honest and consistent. Take great care to assure any children involved that they are not in any way to blame for their elderly relative's memory peculiarities and possible odd behaviour, that this occurrence affects many people without anyone being at fault.

Children may also need particular support and understanding following a bereavement. Often this is difficult for their parents as they can be so wrapped up in their own grief. Special counselling is available for bereaved children. Your community nurse, GP or health visitor should be able to tell you what is available in your area, or ask at the public library.

Why talking can help

Many carers express a desire to simply 'talk to someone' but often they don't know where to start or even whether they ought to be discussing their relative's illness. But talking can be very beneficial, so despite your possible dread of talking about the situation why not overcome your reluctance and at least try talking to each other.

What can be gained by talking? Probably, at least some of the following:

- support for each other;
- comfort and a sense of togetherness;
- reduction of fear and isolation;
- openness and agreement about ground rules for behaviour;
- a sense of perspective;
- a chance to introduce some humour – without being too insensitive;
- clarity and answers to questions;
- regaining and/or retaining a sense of control;
- the sharing of information.
- correction of myths;
- a better chance to find solutions to problems.

The list could be longer – perhaps you and your relative can add some benefits that you have gained by talking about their problems. If you need a listening ear from outside your immediate circle, there are many other people and organisations to whom you can turn for support (see pages 162–175).

How to share feelings

Vera, a carer

'My husband and I are very close and we have never found it difficult to talk about issues – until he began to forget what we had discussed and agreed the previous day. Once I had got over my fear of being the stronger one in the partnership, we both agreed that we would continue to talk about everything as before, but that I might have to go over the topic again, patiently, and accept that it was not his fault.'

There are no rules or special phrases which deal with how to share feelings and make everyone feel less inhibited. But the following guidelines may be useful:

■ Behave in a sensitive and responsible manner, agreeing that matters spoken about privately remain confidential and details will only passed on with express permission. For example, you could say, 'May I share this information with …?'

■ Let your relative set the pace if this feels easier.

■ Acknowledge the open expression of feelings such as tears or anger, and be supportive, but don't attempt to stop the flow of emotion prematurely as most outbursts of this nature tend to subside naturally after the emotion has been vented.

■ If you are having a bad day try to explain what you are feeling and why. For example, 'I feel low today because …' is much easier to understand than a withdrawn manner.

■ Expression of strong emotions is neither right nor wrong. But being offered the opportunity to express emotions is important.

■ Give each other a chance to respond, whether with words or without. A good hug or sitting in shared silence may be sufficient.

■ Don't be frightened of speaking about the past or the future.

■ Accept that your relative's memory loss may make the process of sharing feelings more difficult for them.

For more information

i CRUSE – Bereavement Care (see page 166 for address) offers bereavement counselling for children and adults.

Respite care and practical support

Help is provided to carers by the care services (see Chapter 6). Most care homes offer respite to carers, either through residential admission or a day care service. They are able to offer psychosocial support to carers, and help through the apparent maze of the statutory social services. There are other self-help groups and voluntary organisations offering support to carers in the form of sitting services and specialist support groups.

Practical support is also important. Advice about where to get pieces of equipment sometimes gets overlooked because the professional is focusing on the patient and maybe assumes that the carer knows. Information and practical guidance about such procedures as moving your relative safely are best covered by the appropriate professional at the time of need. Examples of useful caring aids are included in Chapter 6. If you are unsure about where to go for equipment, or feel you do not have the skills to undertake a nursing procedure, do ask for help rather than continue to struggle.

Emergency help and first aid

Carers often express fears about what to do if there is an accident and their relative falls. The advice from the Ambulance Service is to dial 999 for help. Do not attempt to move the person more than is necessary, as they will need to be assessed for injury.

If a situation occurs that needs prompt first aid, try to think and act calmly. You will be more effective and better able to reassure your relative. If your relative falls, collapses or becomes seriously ill, either call an ambulance yourself or ask someone to do this for you. Then treat your relative according to their state of consciousness, until help arrives. If the person is conscious:

- reassure them that help is on the way;
- if they have difficulty breathing or complain of chest pains, gently raise them to a half sitting position, with the head and shoulders supported;
- if they feel faint, make sure they are lying down and encourage them to take a few deep breaths (but not to over-breathe because this can quickly cause dizziness for other reasons);

- do not move a person who has fallen unless you absolutely have to, as this may cause further injury;
- if your relative has diabetes (as well as memory loss) give them a sugary drink or a sugar lump or other sweet food;
- do not give anything to eat or drink if your relative does not have diabetes.

If the person is unconscious:

- if possible, lie them on the floor on their side; otherwise try to position the head with the jaw forwards in order to maintain a clear airway and to prevent saliva and the tongue from falling backwards;
- loosen tight clothing;
- cover the person with a blanket to keep them warm;
- do *not* give any food or fluids of any kind;
- do *not* try to remove dentures because poking about in the mouth of an unconscious person is likely to do more harm than good.

If you become ill or need extra help

If you are ill yourself and need additional help at home during the day, you can contact the duty social services officer or your GP. For assistance outside office hours, contact the social services emergency duty team or a medical answering service. (Look up the numbers in the telephone directory and put them by the telephone now.)

Carer's emergency card

You might be concerned that you could have an accident or be taken ill while you are away from home, leaving the person you care for alone. You can obtain an emergency identity card that gives information about you as a carer so that your relative will not be left unattended. Cards are available from Carers UK (address on page 165).

Carers' advice line

A telephone helpline offering a wide range of information to carers operates nationally for the cost of a local call. Run by Carers UK, lines are open Monday to Friday from 10.00am–12.00 noon, and 2.00–4.00pm. Contact CarersLine on 0808 808 7777.

Emergency help systems

Many local authorities and some charities operate an emergency call system that is linked via the telephone service to specially trained operators (it may not be available to everyone). A charge is usually made to help fund the system, which will vary from area to area. Ask for information at your relative's GP surgery or health centre.

For more information

i Age Concern Factsheet 28 *Information about telephones.*

Fact Box 3

- 1.7 million carers provide care for 20 hours or more every week. 27 per cent of these are aged 65 years or over.

- 70 per cent of those cared for are 65 years or over.

- 6 per cent of people cared for have a mental disability.

- 14 per cent of carers claim to have 'given up work to care'.

- 51 per cent of carers provide personal care to someone within their own home; 22 per cent administer medicines; 71 per cent give other practical help.

Source: Taken from *Facts About Carers*, published by Carers UK, May 2003

Conclusion

This final chapter has offered information and advice to help you focus on your role as a carer and given you an insight into the nature of caring. It has focused more on 'talking-style' support, whereas earlier chapters dealt with everyday affairs and practical issues.

Reading some of this information may have been painful for you, especially if it raised uncomfortable questions you found difficult to answer. If you are one of the many carers who are unfamiliar with the official system, this chapter aims to encourage you to seek support and ask for an assessment of your caring situation. The statistics in the Fact Boxes (3 above and 2 earlier in the chapter) give you a clear indication that you are not alone. Take heart in the fact that the predicament of carers is now under open discussion and their efforts are being increasingly recognised and supported.

For more information

- *ⓘ* Age Concern Factsheet 6 *Finding help at home*.

- *ⓘ* Carers UK acts as the national voice of carers raising awareness and providing support, advice and a range of information booklets (see page 165 for address).

- *ⓘ* Counsel and Care offers free counselling, information and advice for older people and carers, including specialist advice about using independent agencies and the administration of trust funds for single payments such as respite care. (See page 166 for address.)

- *ⓘ* Crossroads – caring for carers – provides respite care (see page 166).

- *ⓘ* Relatives and Residents Association provides advice for the relatives of people in a care home or in hospital long-term. (See page 173 for addresses.)

- *ⓘ* Books are published regularly offering information and support for carers. Check with support organisations for an up-to-date booklist or ask at your local bookshop.

Useful addresses

Age Concern England
1268 London Road
London SW16 4ER
Tel: 020 8765 7200
Website: www.ageconcern.org.uk
See page 177

Alcohol Concern
Waterbridge House
32–36 Loman Street
London SE1 0EE
Tel: 020 7928 7377
Website: www.alcoholconcern.org.uk
Aims to raise awareness of the risk of alcohol abuse and educate peo-ple about safer drinking habits and improve existing services. Provides information only, not direct advice.

Aromatherapy Organisation Council
PO Box 19834
London SE25 6WF
Tel: 020 8251 7912
Website: www.internethealthlibrary.com/Therapies/Aromatherapy/htm
For list of qualified practitioners in your area.

Association of Reflexologists
27 Old Gloucester Street
London WC1N 3XX
Tel: 0870 567 3320
Website: www.aor.org.uk
For names of reflexologists.

Bach Centre

Mount Vernon Ltd.
Bakers Lane
Sotwell
Wallingford
Oxfordshire OX10 0PX
Tel: 01491 834678
Website: www.bachcentre.com/centre
For list of trained practitioners and details of publications, tapes and educational material.

British Association for Counselling and Psychotherapy

1 Regent Place
Rugby
Warwickshire CV21 2PJ
Helpline: 0870 443 5252
Website: www.bacp.co.uk
Publishes a directory of counsellors and psychotherapists in the UK.

British Complementary Medicine Association (BCMA)

249 Fosse Road South
Leicester LE3 1AE
Tel: 0116 282 5511
Website: www.bcma.co.uk
Publishes BCMA National Practitioner Register listing practitioners who belong to member organisations.

British Herbal Medicine Association (BHMA)

Sun House
Church Street
Stroud
Gloucester GL5 1JL
Tel: 01453 751389
Website: www.bhma.info
Provides an information service and list of qualified herbal practitioners.

British Holistic Medical Association (BHMA)

59 Lansdowne Place
Hove
East Sussex BN3 1FL
Tel: 01273 725951
Website: www.bhma-sec.dircon.co.uk
For directory of members and book/tape list.

British Homeopathic Association (BHA)

Hahneman House
29 Park Street West
Luton LU1 3BE
Tel: 08704 443950
Website: www.trust.homeopathy.org
Provides an information service, newsletter, book list and names of homeopathic practitioners.

British Medical Association (BMA)

BMA House
Tavistock Square
London WC1H 9JP
Tel: 020 7387 4499
Fax: 020 7387 6400
Email: info.web@bma.org.uk
Website: www.bma.org.uk
The professional organisation and 'voice' for all doctors from all branches of medicine in the UK. Information is also available for non-medical people.

BNA (British Nursing Association)

North Place
82 Great North Road
Hatfield
Hertfordshire AL9 5BL
Tel: 01707 263544
Website: www.bnauk.com
For respite and nursing care.

British Red Cross

9 Grosvenor Crescent
London SW1X 7EJ
Tel: 020 7235 5454
Or look in the telephone directory for a local contact number.
For advice about arranging for equipment on loan.

Care and Repair England

3rd Floor
Bridgford House
Pavilion Road
West Bridgford
Nottingham NG2 5GJ
Tel: 0115 982 1527
Website: www.careandrepair-england.org.uk
Advice and practical assistance to older and disabled people and those on low incomes, to help them improve their home conditions.

Carers UK

20–25 Glasshouse Yard
London EC1A 4JS
Tel: 020 7490 8818
CarersLine: 0808 808 7777
Website: www.carersonline.org.uk
Acts as the national voice of carers, raising awareness and providing support, information and advice.

Centre for Study of Complementary Medicine

51 Bedford Place
Southampton SO15 2DT
Tel: 023 8033 4752
For advice and details of specialist organisations.

Community Transport Association

Highbank
Halton Street
Hyde

Cheshire SK14 2NY
Tel: 0161 351 1475
Advice: 0161 367 8780
Services to benefit providers of transport for people with mobility problems. Also keeps a database of all Dial-a-Ride schemes.

Consumers' Association
2 Marylebone Road
London NW1 4DF
Tel: 0845 307 4000
Website: www.which.net
For advice about consumer issues and rights.

Counsel and Care
Lower Ground Floor
Twyman House
16 Bonny Street
London NW1 9PG
Tel: 020 7485 1566
Website: www.counselandcare.org.uk
Offers free counselling, information and advice for older people and carers, including specialist advice about using independent agencies and the administration of trust funds for single payments (eg respite care).

Crossroads Care
10 Regent Place
Rugby
Warwickshire CV21 2PN
Tel: 01788 573653
Website: www.crossroads.org.uk
For a range of services, including personal and respite care.

CRUSE – Bereavement Care
126 Sheen Road
Richmond
Surrey TW9 1UR

Tel: 020 8940 4818
Website: www.crusebereavementcare.org.uk
For all types of bereavement counselling and a wide range of publications.

Depression Alliance (England)

35 Westminster Bridge Road
London SE1 7JB
Tel: 020 7633 0557
Textphone: 020 7928 9992
Website: www.depressionalliance.org
Provides information, support and understanding to everyone affected by depression and campaigns to raise awareness of the illness.

Depression Alliance (Scotland)

3 Grosvenor Gardens
Edinburgh EH12 5JU
Tel: 0131 467 3050

Depression Alliance (Cymru)

11 Plas Melin
Westbourne Road
Whitchurch
Cardiff CF4 2BT
Tel: 029 2069 2891

Disabled Living Centres Council

Redbank House
4 St Chads Street
Manchester M8 8QA
Tel: 0161 834 1044
Website: www.dlce.org.uk
For Disabled Living Centres nearest you, where you can see aids and equipment.

Disabled Living Foundation
380–384 Harrow Road
London W9 2HU
Tel: 020 7289 6111
Equipment helpline: 0870 603 9177
Minicom: 0879 603 9176
Website: www.dlf.org.uk
*Information and advice about all aspects of daily living (and aids) for
people with disability.*

Disabled Persons Railcard Office
PO Box 1YT
Newcastle-upon-Tyne NE99 1YT
Helpline: 0191 269 0303
*For railcard offering concessionary fares. An application form and use-
ful booklet called Rail Travel for Disabled Passengers can be found at
most larger stations or from address above.*

Drinkline
7th Floor, Weddell House
13–14 Smithfield
London EC1A 9DL
Tel: 020 7332 0202
*National Alcohol helpline that provides confidential information, help
and advice about drinking to anyone, including people worried about
someone else's drinking.*

Elderly Accommodation Counsel
3rd Floor
89 Albert Embankment
London SE1 7TP
Tel: 020 7820 1343
Fax: 020 7820 3970
Website: www.housingcare.org.uk
*Computerised information about all forms of accommodation for older
people (including nursing homes and hospices) and advice on top-up
funding.*

EXTEND

22 Maltings Drive
Wheathampstead
Hertfordshire AL4 8QJ
Tel/Fax: 01582 832760
Provides exercise in the form of movement to music for people over 60 years and less able people of all ages.

Federation of Independent Advice Centres

4 Dean's Court
St Paul's Churchyard
London EC4V 5AA
Tel: 020 7489 1800
Promotes the provision of independent advice services in the UK.

Help the Aged

207–221 Pentonville Road
London N1 9UZ
Tel: 020 7278 1114
Email: info@helptheaged.org.uk
Website: www.helptheaged.org.uk
Advice and support for older people and their carers.

HELPBOX

The Help for Health Trust
Freepost
Winchester SO22 5BR
Tel: 01962 849100
A computer database that holds a vast and comprehensive range of health-related information.

Homeopathic Trust

2 Powis Place
Great Ormond Street
London WC1N 3HT
Tel: 020 7837 9469
For the names of homeopathic trained doctors.

Independent Healthcare Association
22 Little Russell Street
London WC1A 2HT
Tel: 020 7430 0837
Website: www.iha.org.uk
For information about finding and paying for residential and nursing home care.

Institute of Complementary Medicine (ICM)
PO Box 194
London SE16 7QZ
Tel: 020 7237 5165
Advice and details of specialist organisations.

International Federation of Aromatherapists
182 Chiswick High Road
London W4 1PP
Tel: 020 8742 2605
For a book list and details of qualified practitioners in your area.

International Federation of Reflexologists
78 Edridge Road
Croydon
Surrey CR0 1EF
Tel: 020 8667 9454
For names of qualified reflexologists in your area.

International Society of Aromatherapists
ISPA House
82 Ashby Road
Hinckley
Leicestershire LE10 1SN
Tel: 01455 637987
For a book list and details of qualified practitioners in your area.

Jewish Care
Stewart Young House
221 Golders Green Road

London NW11 9DQ
Tel: 020 8458 3282
Social care, personal support and residential homes for Jewish people.

MIND (National Association for Mental Health)

Granta House
15–19 Broadway
London E15 4BQ
Tel: 0847 660 163 (Monday–Friday, 9.15am–4.45pm)
Website: www.mind.org.uk
Information service for all matters relating to mental health.

MIND Cymru

23 St Mary's Street
Cardiff CF1 2AA
Tel: 029 2039 5123

Motability

Gate House, West Gate
Harlow
Essex CM20 1HR
Helpline: 01279 635666
Advice about cars, scooters and wheelchairs for disabled people.

National Association of Councils for Voluntary Service

3rd Floor, Arundel Court
177 Arundel Street
Sheffield S1 2NU
Tel: 0114 278 6636
Promotes and supports the work of councils for voluntary service.

National College of Hypnosis and Psychotherapy

12 Cross Street
Nelson
Lancashire BB9 7EN
Tel: 01282 699378
Publishes an annual directory of practitioners.

National Federation of Spiritual Healers

Old Manor Farm Studio
Church Street
Sunbury on Thames
Middlesex TW16 6RG
Tel: 0891 616080 (premium rate line)
Advice and details of spiritual healers.

New World Aurora

16A Neal's Yard
Covent Garden
London WC2H 9DP
Tel: 020 7379 5972
For catalogue of relaxation music tapes.

NHS Direct

Tel: 0845 46 47
Website: www.nhsdirect.nhs.uk
A 24-hour nurse-led helpline providing confidential healthcare advice and information.

NHS Smoking Helpline

Tel: 0800 169 0169
Offers help and support to give up all forms of smoking.

No Panic

Tel: 0800 783 1531
Telephone service only for an information pack about dealing with anxiety and panic. Callers are asked to leave details of their name and address on an answerphone as the organisation cannot return calls.

Northern Ireland Association for Mental Health

80 University Street
Belfast BT7 1HE
Tel: 28 9032 8474
A voluntary organisation providing services for people with mental health needs, including residential and day care, counselling, information, education and training.

172

Public Guardianship Office
Protection Division
Archway Tower
2 Junction Road
London N19 5SZ
Tel: 020 7664 7300/7000/7208
Enquiry Line: 0845 330 2900
Advice about powers of attorney.

Quitline
Tel: 0800 002 200
Website: www.quit.org.uk
A freephone helpline that provides confidential and practical advice for people wanting to give up smoking.

RADAR (Royal Association for Disability and Rehabilitation)
12 City Forum
250 City Road
London EC1V 8AF
Tel: 020 7250 3222
Information about aids and mobility, holidays and leisure.

Relatives & Residents Association
5 Tavistock Place
London WC1H 9SN
Tel: 020 7916 6055
Website: www.relres.org.uk
Offers information, practical advice and a forum for discussion and engagement to people entering long term care, and their relatives.

Research Institute for Consumer Affairs (RICA)
2 Marylebone Road
London NW1 4DF
Tel: 020 7830 7679
Tests and evaluates goods and services for disabled and older people, including ordinary consumer products as well as special aids and equipment.

The Samaritans
46 Marshall Street
London W1V 1LR
Tel: 08457 90 90 90
Textphone: 08457 90 91 92 (24 hours every day)
Offers confidential emotional support to any person who is suicidal or despairing.

The Scottish Association for Mental Health
Cumbrae House
15 Carlton Court
Glasgow G5 9JP
Tel: 0141 568 7000
Offers confidential support, information and advice to any person suffering from a mental health illness, including other people affected by the illness.

St John Ambulance
Look in the telephone directory for local contact number.
For advice about arranging equipment on loan and first aid courses.

Society of Homeopaths
4A Artizan Road
Northampton NN1 4HU
Tel: 01604 621400
For names of homeopathic practitioners.

Sports Council
16 Upper Woburn Place
London WC1H 0QP
Tel: 020 7263 1500
Provides general information about all sports.

Stress Management Training Institute
Foxhills
30 Victoria Avenue
Shanklin
Isle of Wight PO37 6LS

Tel: 01983 868166
Publishes a wide range of materials to help reduce stress: leaflets, audio tapes, books and newsletter.

Tripscope
The Vassall Centre
Gill Avenue
Bristol BS16 2QQ
Tel/Textphone: 08457 585641
A national travel and transport information service for older and disabled people.

UK College of Complementary Health Care Studies
St Charles Hospital
Exmoor Street
London W10 6DZ
Tel: 020 8964 1205
For a list of qualified practitioners of therapeutic massage.

UK Homeopathic Medical Association
6 Livingstone Road
Gravesend
Kent DA12 5DZ
Tel: 01474 560336
For the names of homeopathic practitioners.

United Kingdom Home Care Association (UKHCA)
42B Banstead Road
Carshalton Beeches
Surrey SM5 3NW
Tel: 020 8288 1551
For information about organisations providing home care in your area.

University of the Third Age (U3A)
National Office
26 Harrison Street
London WC1H 8JG
Tel: 020 7837 8838

Day-time study and recreational classes. Send a sae for further information about classes for older people, or look in the telephone directory for local branch.

Vehicle Excise Duty (Road Tax)
DLA Unit
Warbreck House
Warbreck Hill Road
Blackpool FY2 0YE
Tel: 08457 123456
Information about exemption from road tax for vehicles used exclusively by or for disabled people.

Volunteer Development England
(Formerly National Association of Volunteer Bureaux)
New Oxford House
16 Waterloo Street
Birmingham B2 5UG
Tel: 0121 633 4555
Information on matters related to volunteering, with a directory of volunteer bureaux and other publications.

Winged Fellowship Trust
Angel House
20–32 Pentonville Road
London N1 9XD
Tel: 020 7833 2594
Website: www.wft.org.uk
Provides respite care and holidays for physically disabled people, with or without a partner.

About Age Concern

This book is one of a wide range of publications produced by Age Concern England, the National Council on Ageing. Age Concern works on behalf of all older people and believes later life should be fulfilling and enjoyable. For too many this is impossible. As the leading charitable movement in the UK concerned with ageing and older people, Age Concern finds effective ways to change that situation.

Where possible, we enable older people to solve problems themselves, providing as much or as little support as they need. A network of local Age Concerns, supported by many thousands of volunteers, provides community-based services such as lunch clubs, day centres and home visiting.

Nationally, we take a lead role in campaigning, parliamentary work, policy analysis, research, specialist information and advice provision, and publishing. Innovative programmes promote healthier lifestyles and provide older people with opportunities to give the experience of a lifetime back to their communities.

Age Concern is dependent on donations, covenants and legacies.

Age Concern England
1268 London Road
London SW16 4ER
Tel: 020 8765 7200
Fax: 020 8765 7211
Website: www.ageconcern.org.uk

Age Concern Scotland
113 Rose Street
Edinburgh EH2 3D
Tel: 0131 220 3345
Fax: 0131 220 2779
Website:
www.ageconcernscotland.org.uk

Age Concern Cymru
4th Floor
1 Cathedral Road
Cardiff CF11 9SD
Tel: 029 2037 1566
Fax: 029 2039 9562
Website:www.accymru.org.uk

Age Concern Northern Ireland
3 Lower Crescent
Belfast BT7 1NR
Tel: 028 9024 5729
Fax: 028 9023 5497
Website: www.ageconcernni.org

Other books in this series

Caring for someone with depression
Toni Battison
£6.99 0-86242-389-9

Caring for someone with cancer
Toni Battison
£6.99 0-86242-382-1

Caring for someone with a heart problem
Toni Battison
£6.99 0-86242-371-6

The Carer's Handbook: What to do and who to turn to
Marina Lewycka
£6.99 0-86242-366-X

Choices for the carer of an elderly relative
Marina Lewycka
£6.99 0-86242-375-9

Caring for someone with diabetes
Marina Lewycka
£6.99 0-86242-374-0

Caring for someone with a sight problem
Marina Lewycka
£6.99 0-86242-381-3

Caring for someone with a hearing loss
Marina Lewycka
£6.99 0-86242-380-5

Caring for someone who is dying
Penny Mares
£6.99 0-86242-370-8

Caring for someone with arthritis
Jim Pollard
£6.99 0-86242-373-2

Caring for someone at a distance
Julie Spencer-Cingöz
£6.99 0-86242-367-8

Caring for someone who has had a stroke
Philip Coyne with Penny Mares
£6.99 0-86242-369-4

Caring for someone with an alcohol problem
Mike Ward
£6.99 0-86242-372-4

Caring for someone with dementia
Jane Brotchie
£6.99 0-86242-368-6

Publications from Age Concern Books

Your Rights: A guide to money benefits for older people

Sally West

A highly acclaimed annual guide to the State benefits available to older people. It contains current information on Income Support, Housing Benefit and retirement pensions, among other matters, and provides advice on how to claim.

For more information, please telephone 0870 44 22 120.

Their Rights: Advance directives and living wills explored

Kevin Kendrick and Simon Robinson

In a world of uncertainty, death is certain. For some people, dying can be an undignified and demeaning process that robs them of choice and individuality. In recent decades, 'living wills' or ' advance directives' have been actively promoted as a means of giving people some pre-emptive choice about medical treatment.

This book provides a focused and informative account of the key issues surrounding this debate, and looks at the practical issues involved in drawing up an advance directive.

£9.99 0-86242-244-2

If you would like to order any of these titles, please write to the address below, enclosing a cheque or money order for the appropriate amount (plus £1.99 p&p for one book; for additional books please add 75p per book up to a maximum of £7.50) made payable to Age Concern England. Credit card orders may be made on 0870 44 22 120. Books can also be ordered online at www.ageconcern.org.uk/shop

Age Concern Books
Units 5 and 6
Industrial Estate
Brecon
Powys LD3 8LA

Bulk order discounts

Age Concern Books is pleased to offer a discount on orders totalling 50 or more copies of the same title. For details, please contact Age Concern Books on Tel: 0870 44 22 120.

Customised editions

Age Concern Books is pleased to offer a free 'customisation' service for anyone wishing to purchase 500 or more copies of the title. This gives you the option to have a unique front cover design featuring your organisation's logo and corporate colours, or adding your logo to the current cover design. You can also insert an additional four pages of text for a small additional fee. Existing clients include many of the biggest names in British industry, retailing and finance, the Trades Union Movement, educational establishments, the statutory and voluntary sectors, and welfare associations. For full details, please contact Sue Henning, Age Concern Books, Astral House, 1268 London Road, London SW16 4ER. Tel: 020 8765 7200. Fax: 020 8765 7211. Email: hennins@ace.org.uk

Visit our Website at: www.ageconcern.org.uk/shop

Age Concern Information Line/ Factsheets subscription

Age Concern produces 44 comprehensive factsheets designed to answer many of the questions older people (or those advising them) may have. These include money and benefits, health, community care, leisure and education, and housing. For up to five free factsheets, telephone: 0800 00 99 66 (7am–7pm, seven days a week, every day of the year). Alternatively you may prefer to write to Age Concern, FREEPOST (SWB 30375), Ashburton, Devon TQ13 7ZZ.

For professionals working with older people, the factsheets are available on an annual subscription service, which includes updates throughout the year. For further details and costs of the subscription, please write to Age Concern at the above Freepost address.

We hope that this publication has been useful to you. If so, we would very much like to hear from you. Alternatively, if you feel that we could add or change anything, then please write and tell us, using the following Freepost address: Age Concern, FREEPOST CN1794, London SW16 4BR

Index